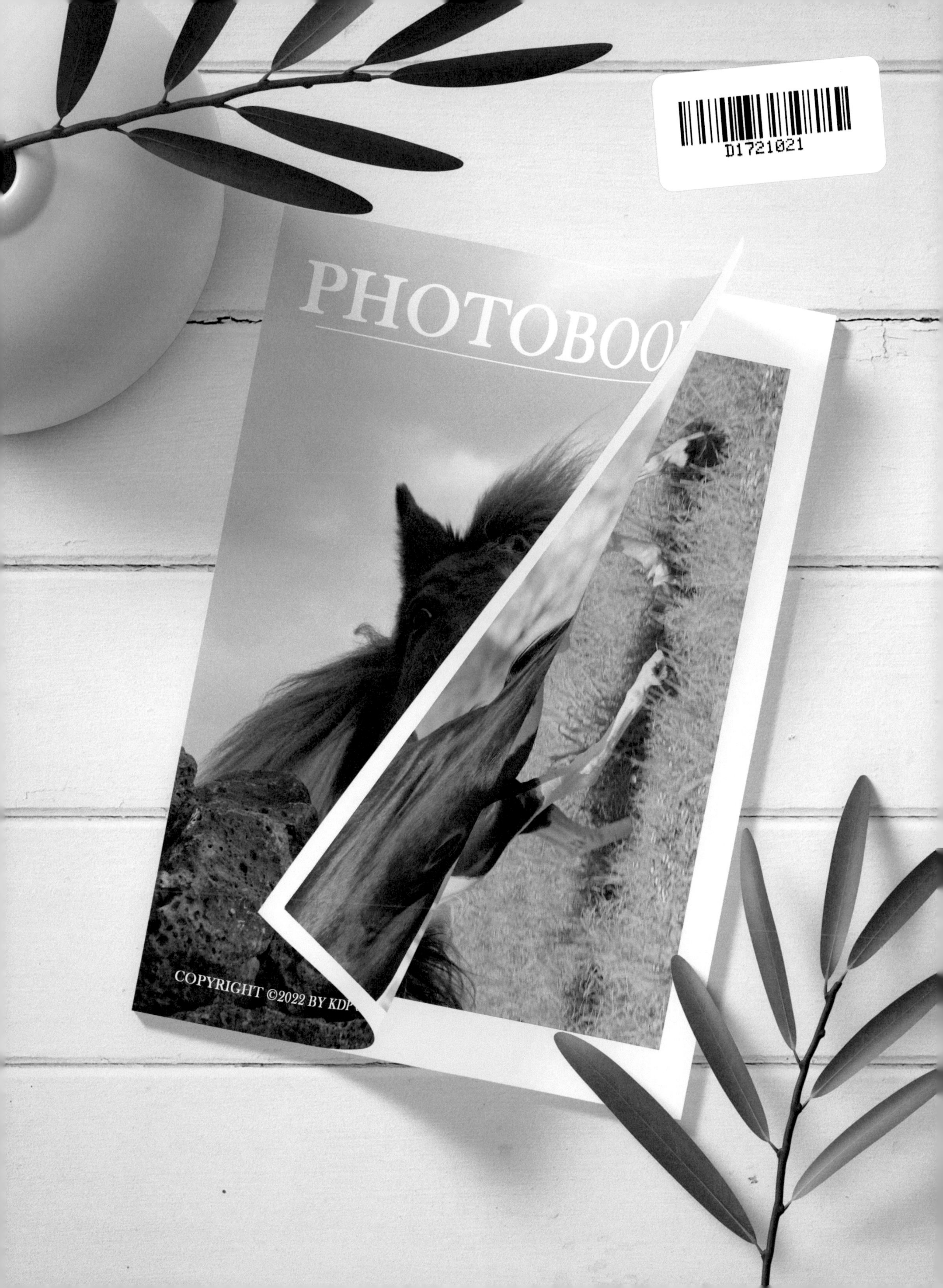
PHOTOBOO
COPYRIGHT ©2022 BY KDP

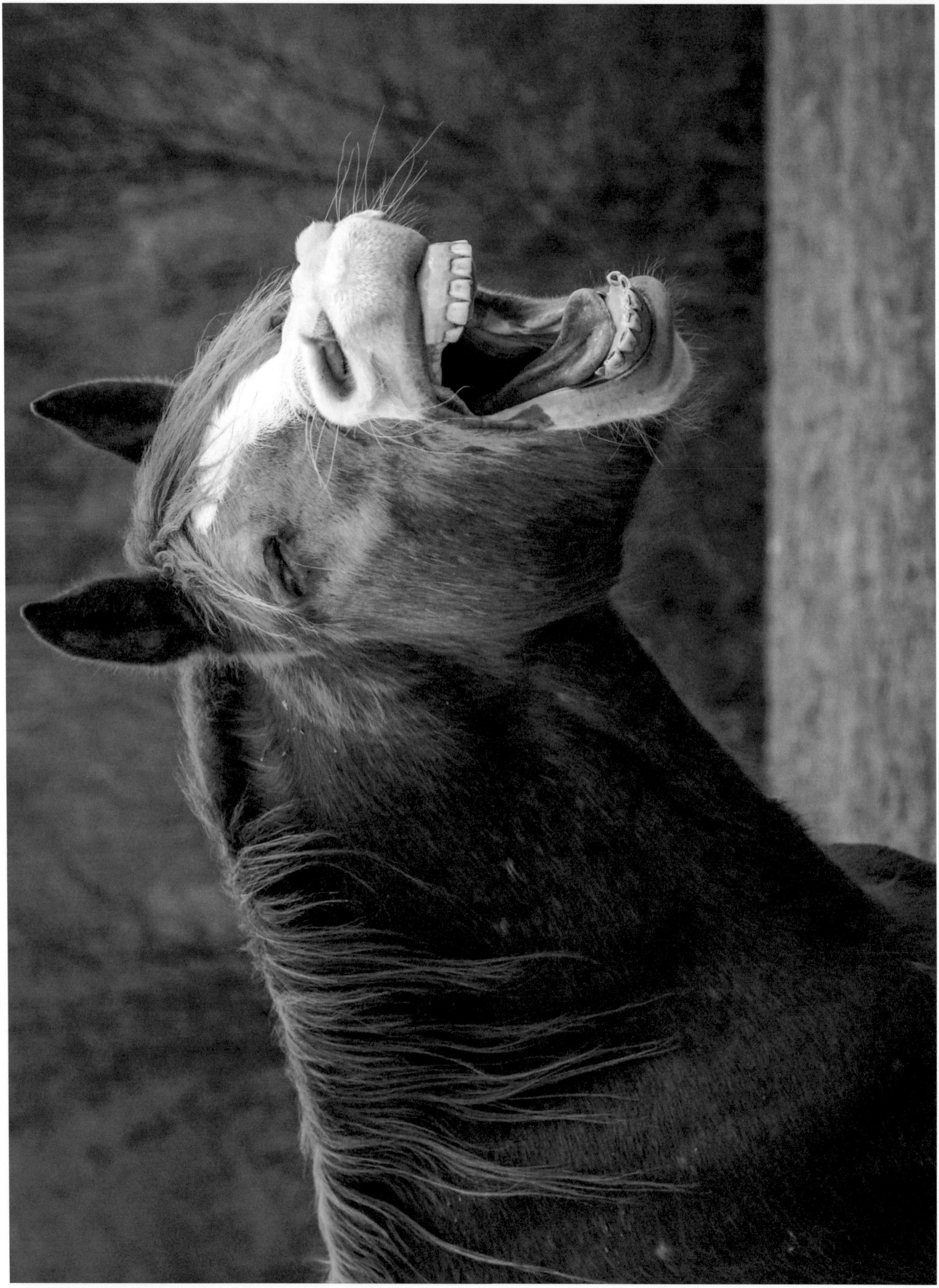

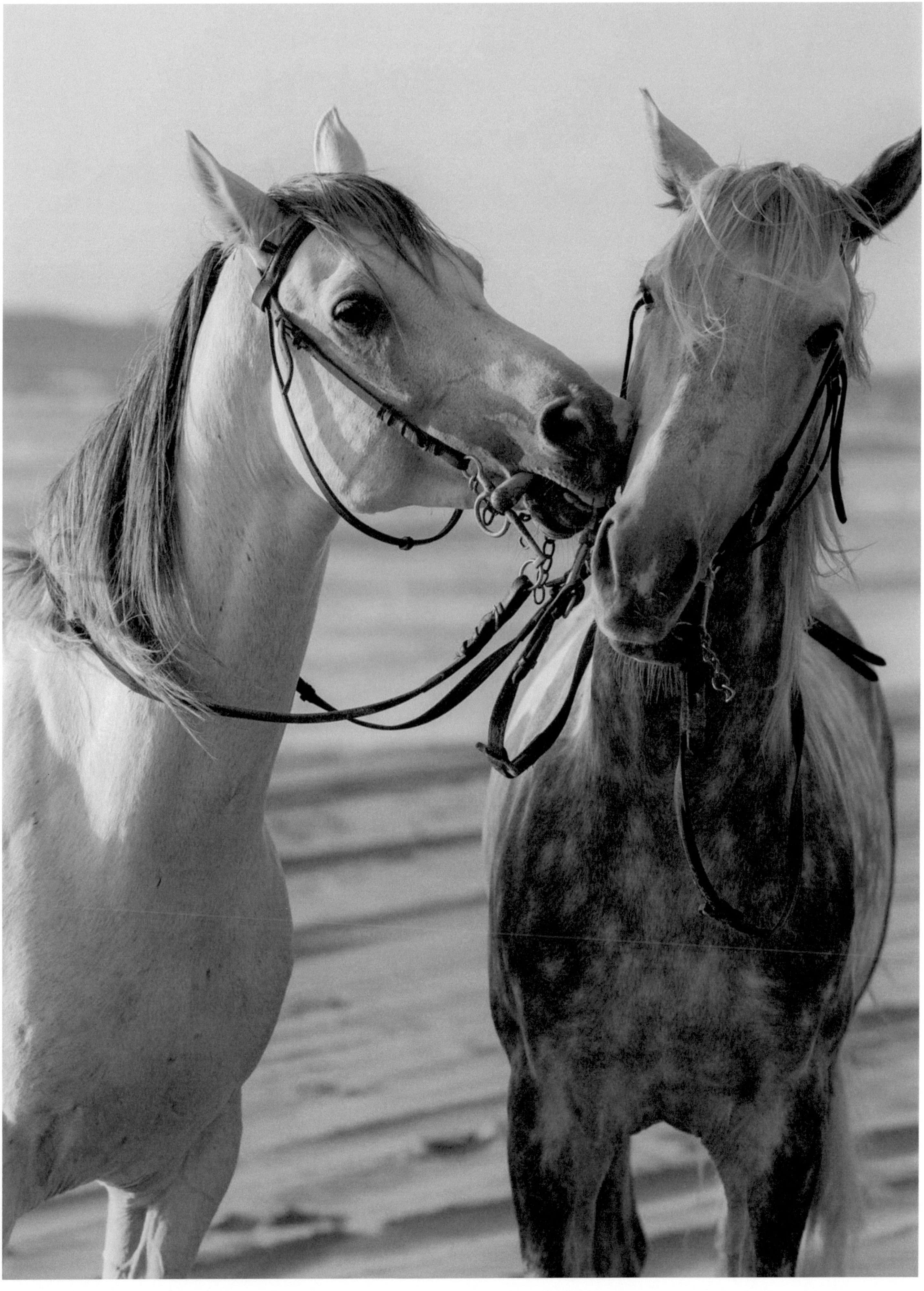

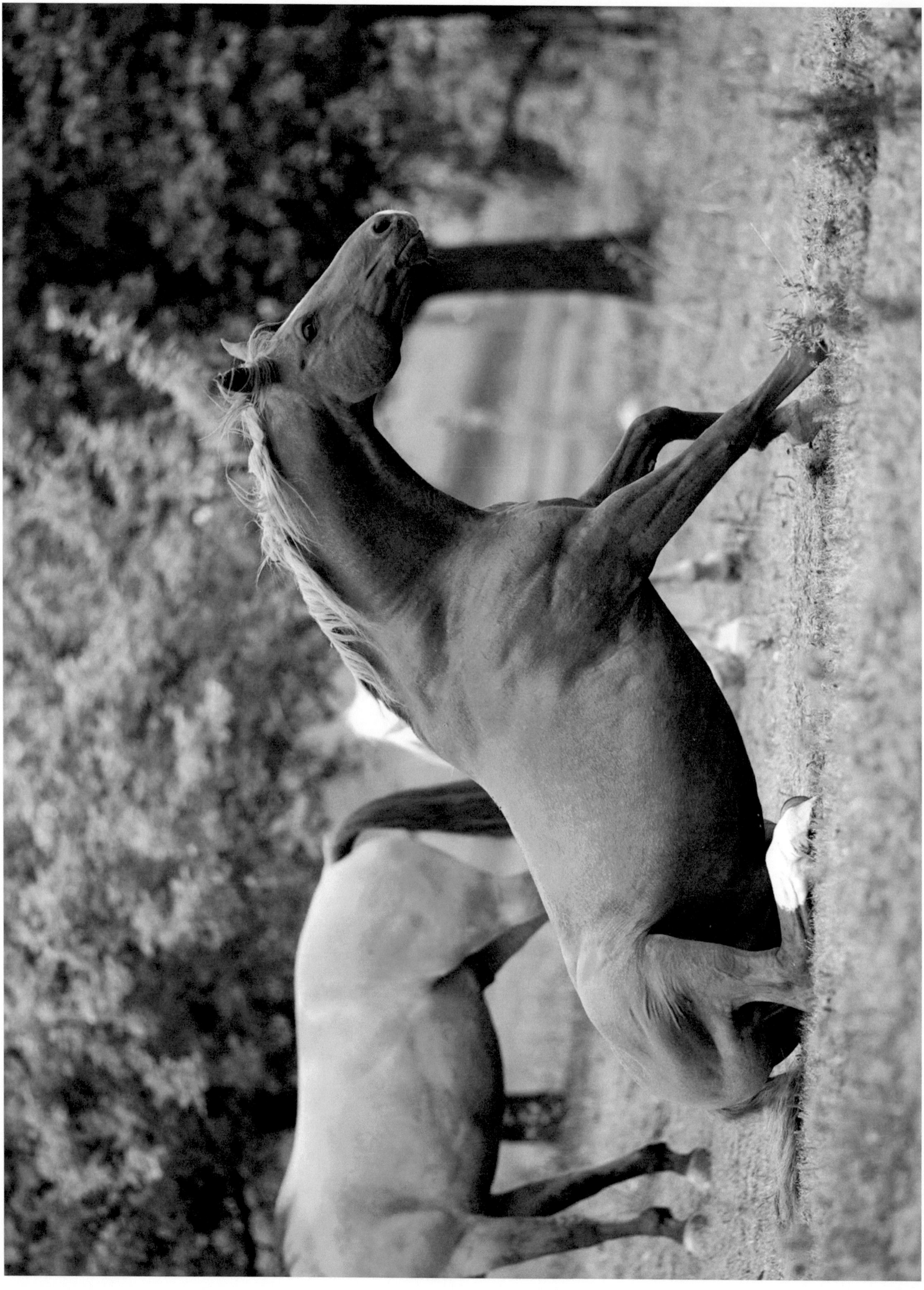

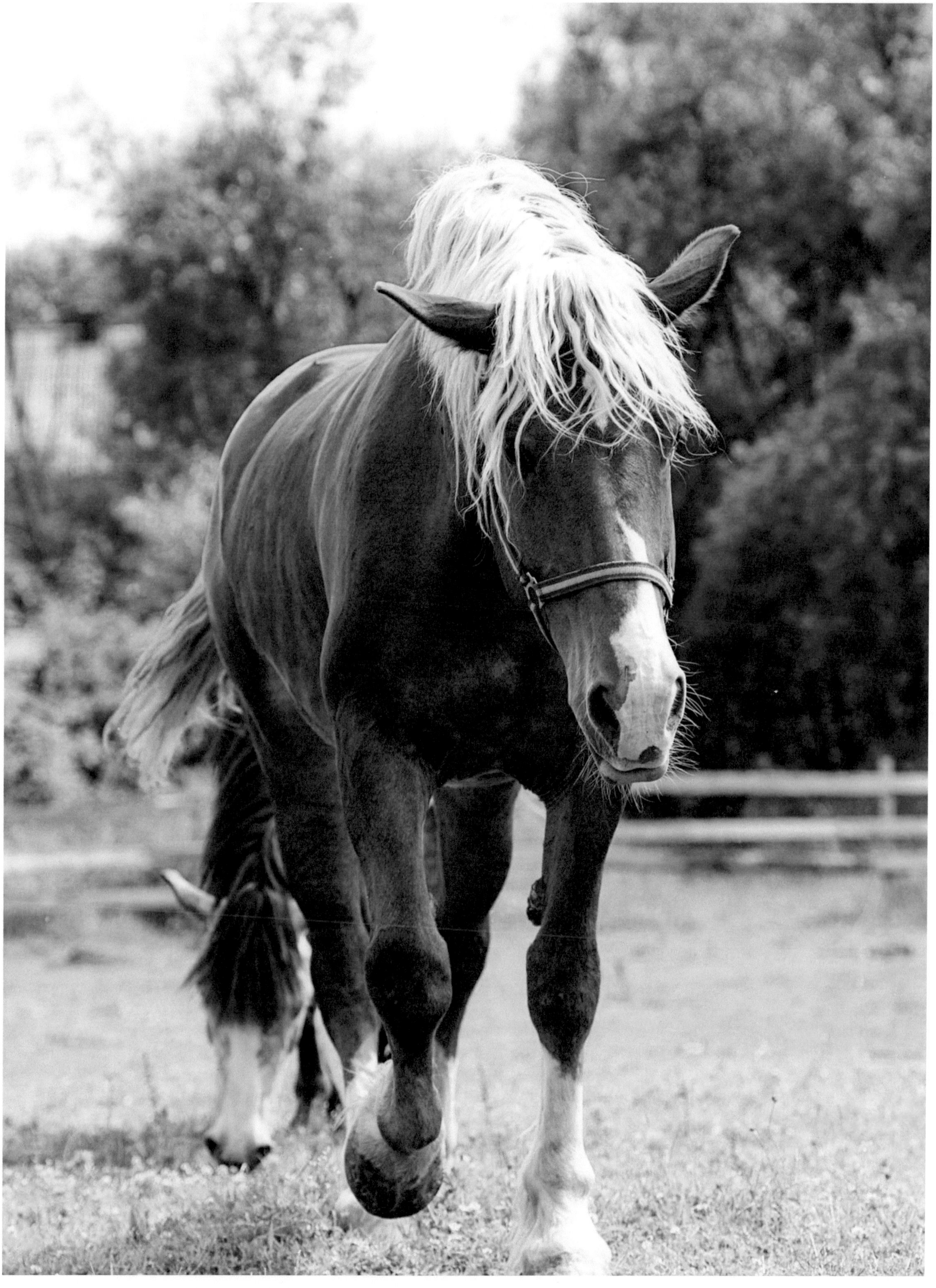

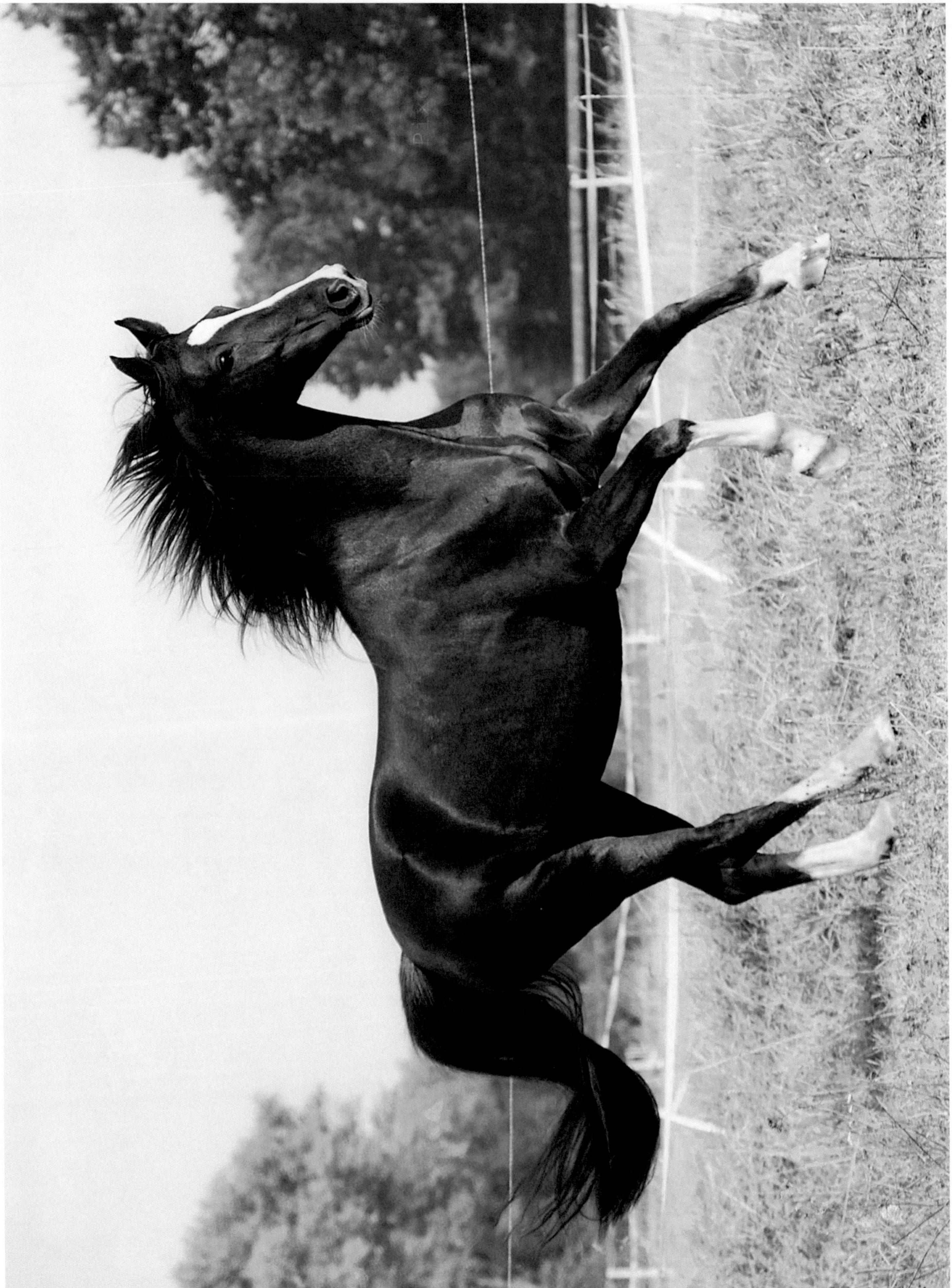

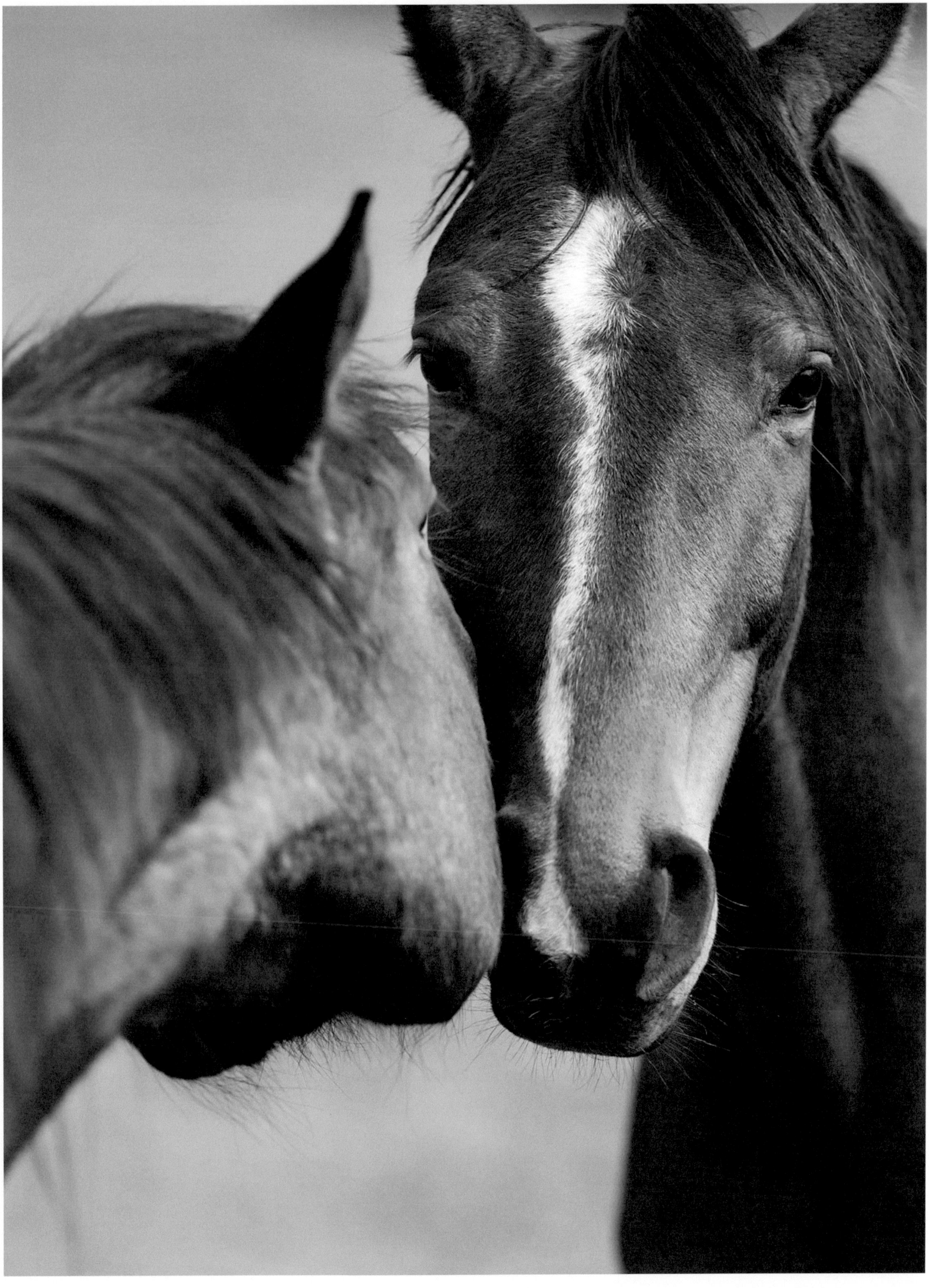

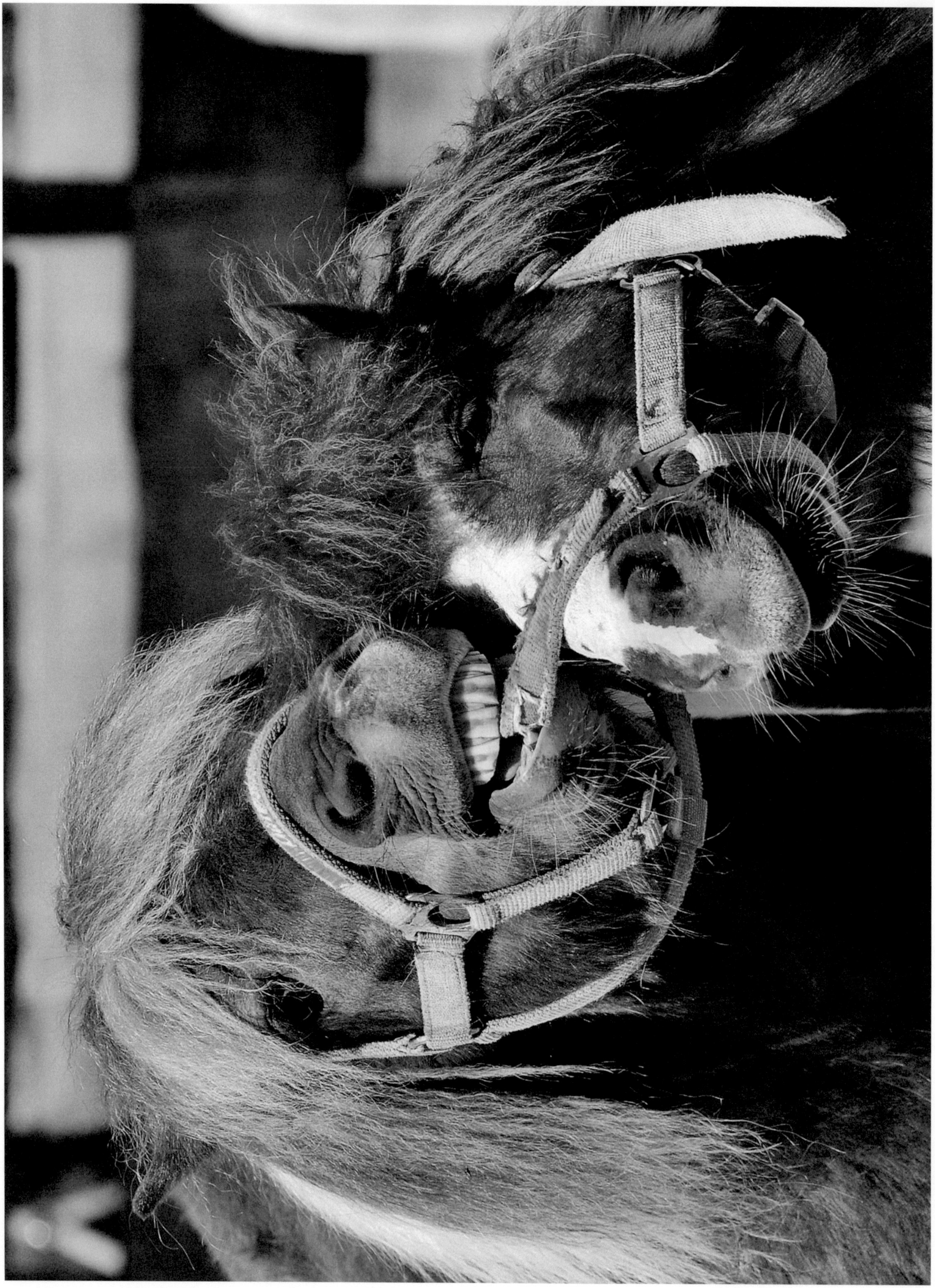

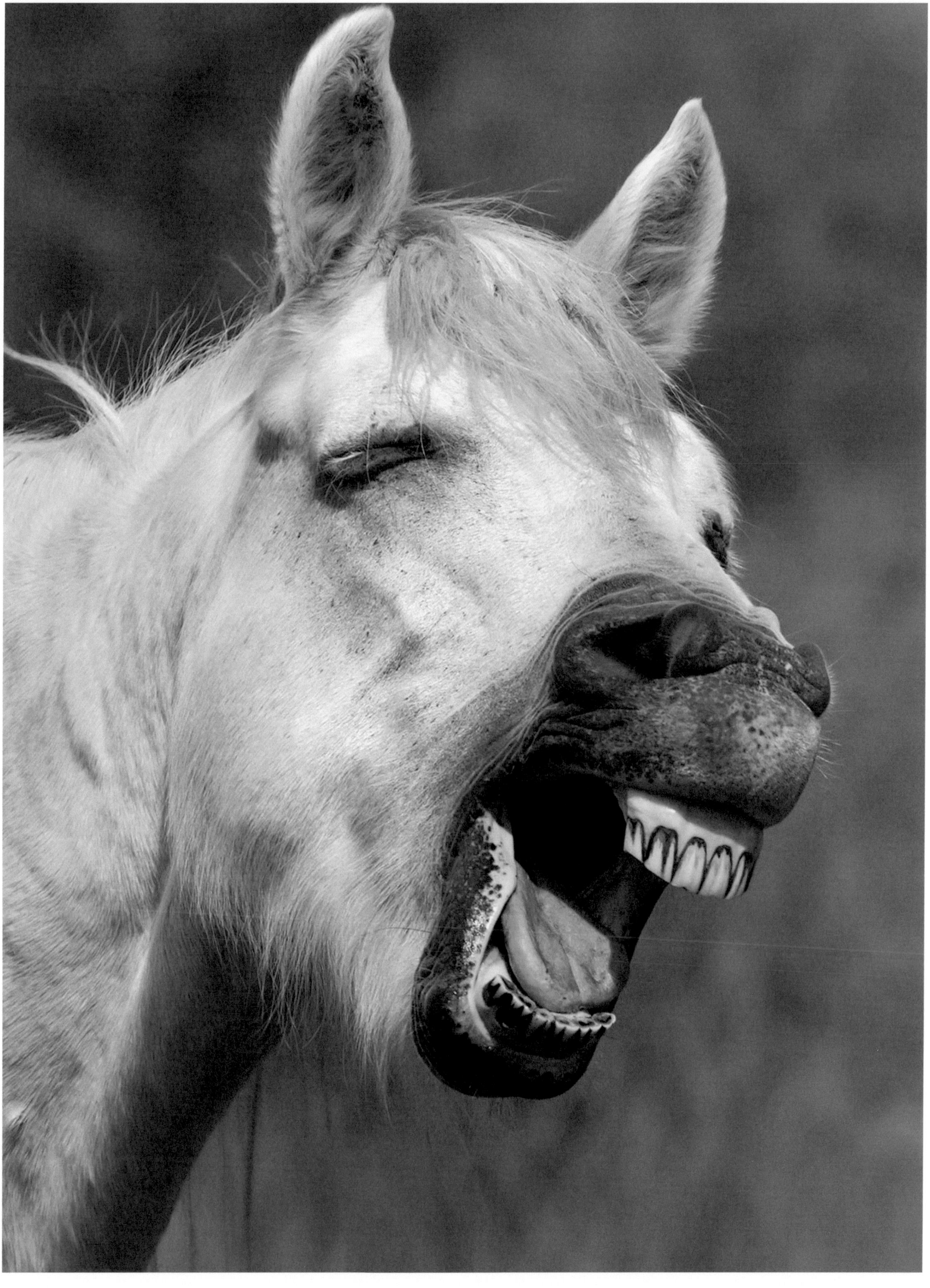

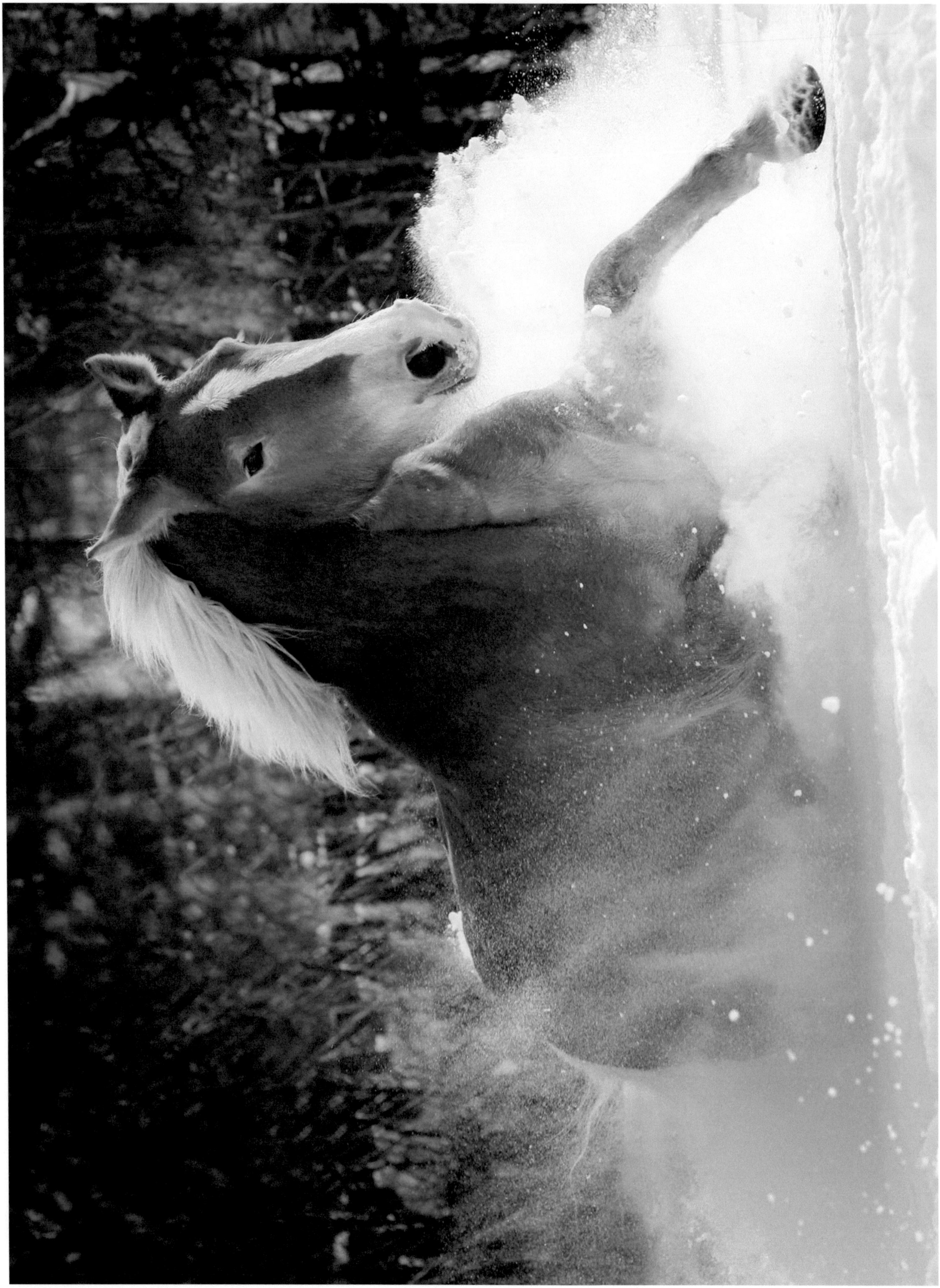

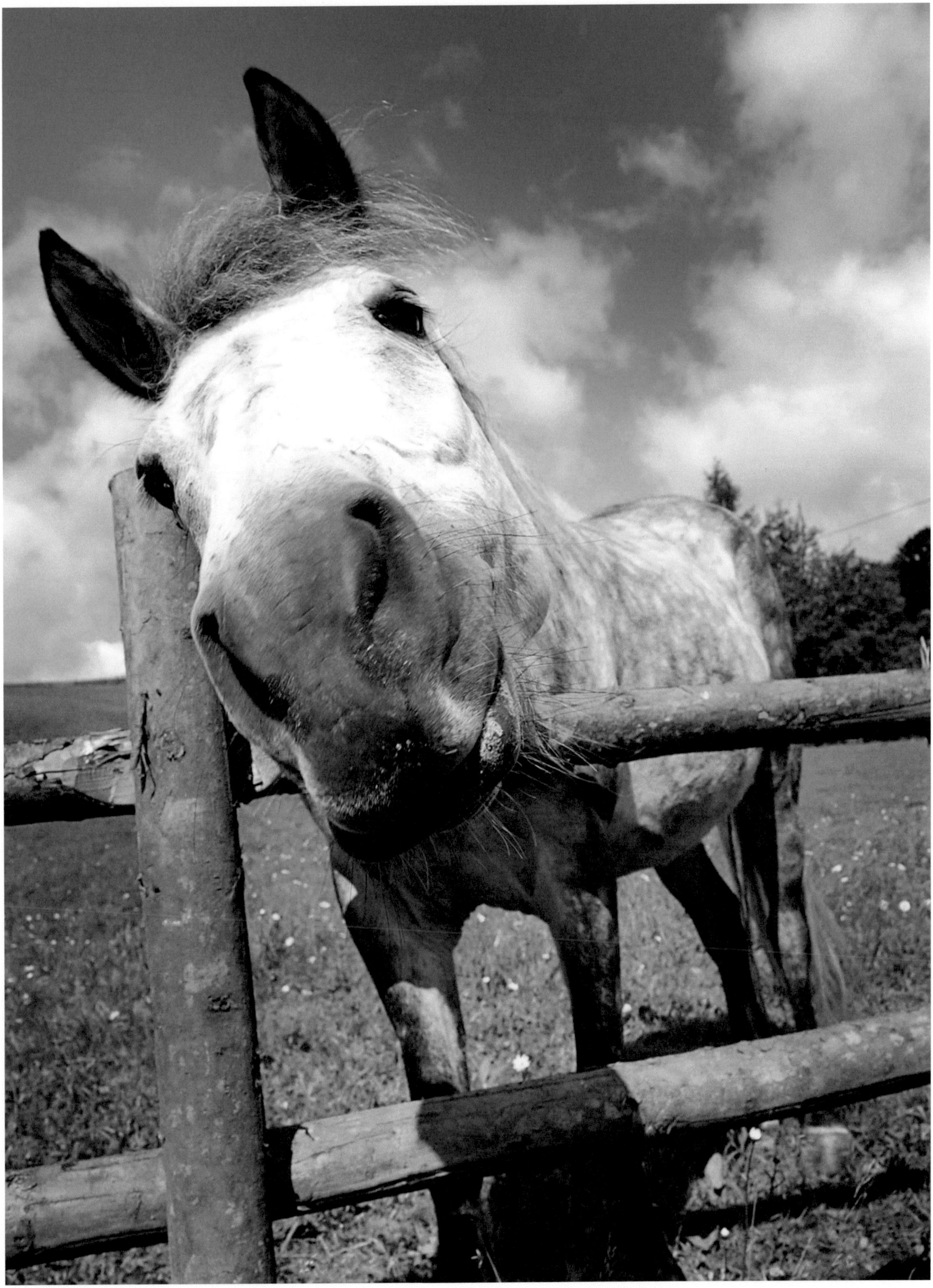

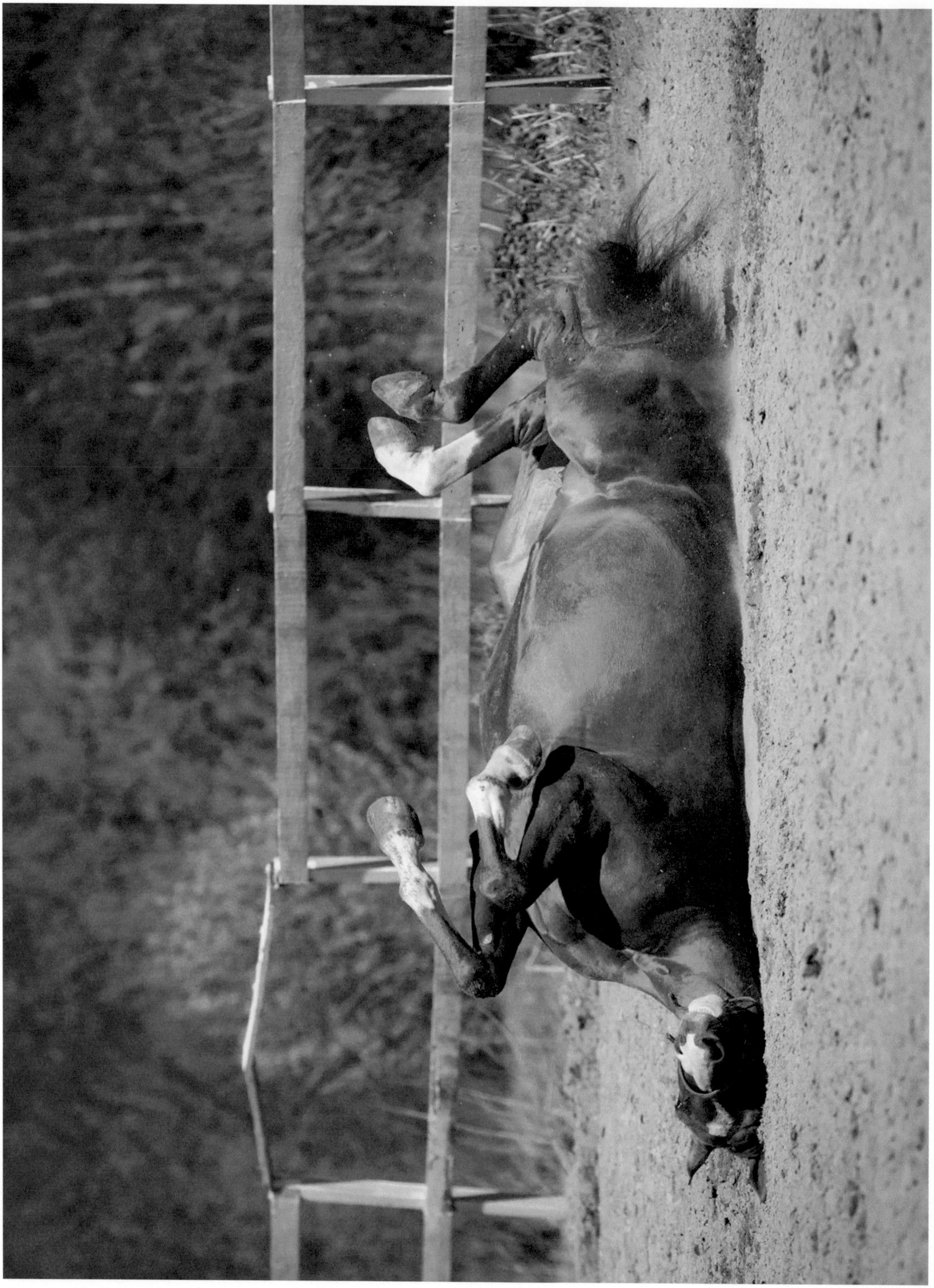

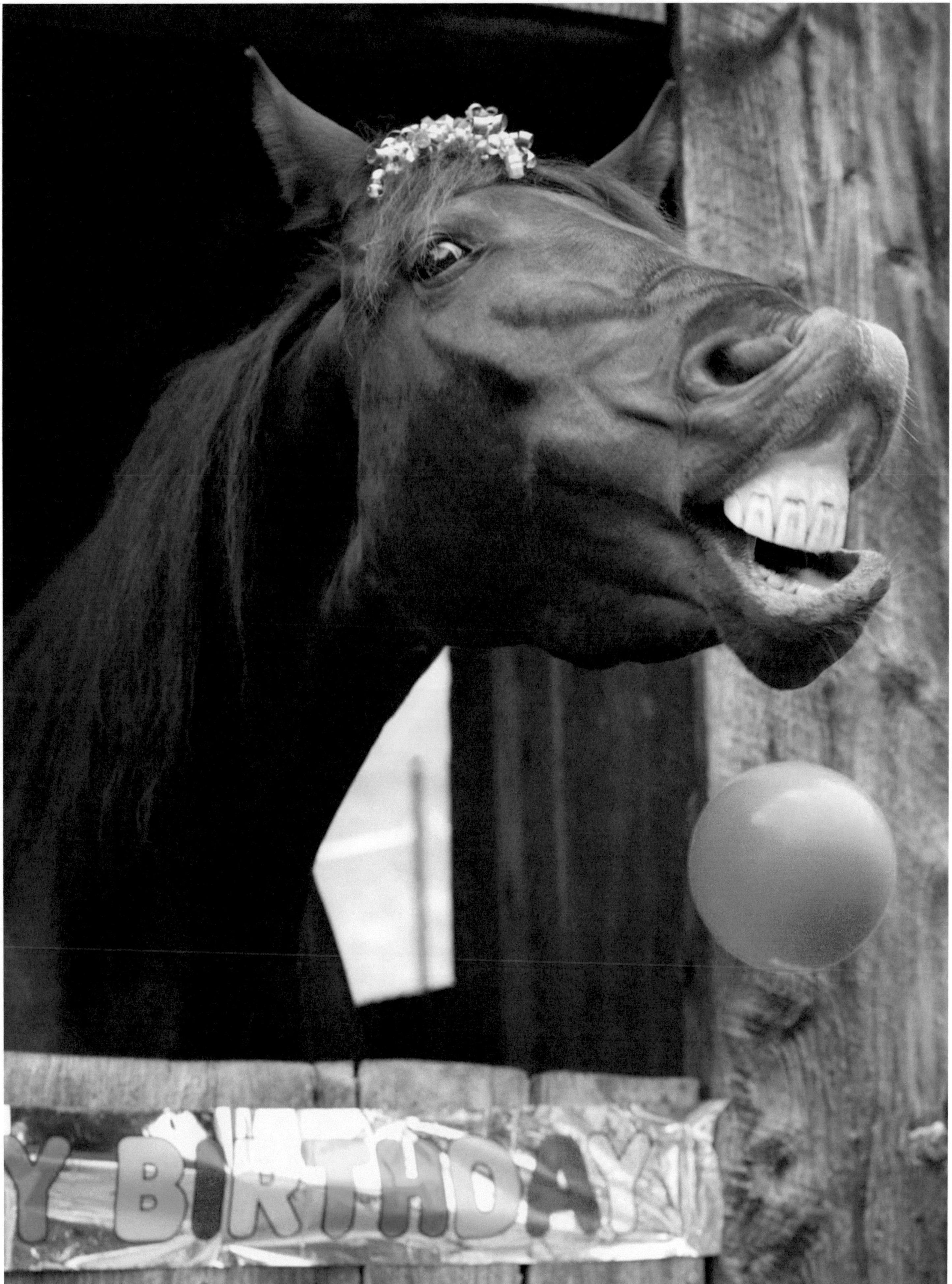
BIRTHDAY

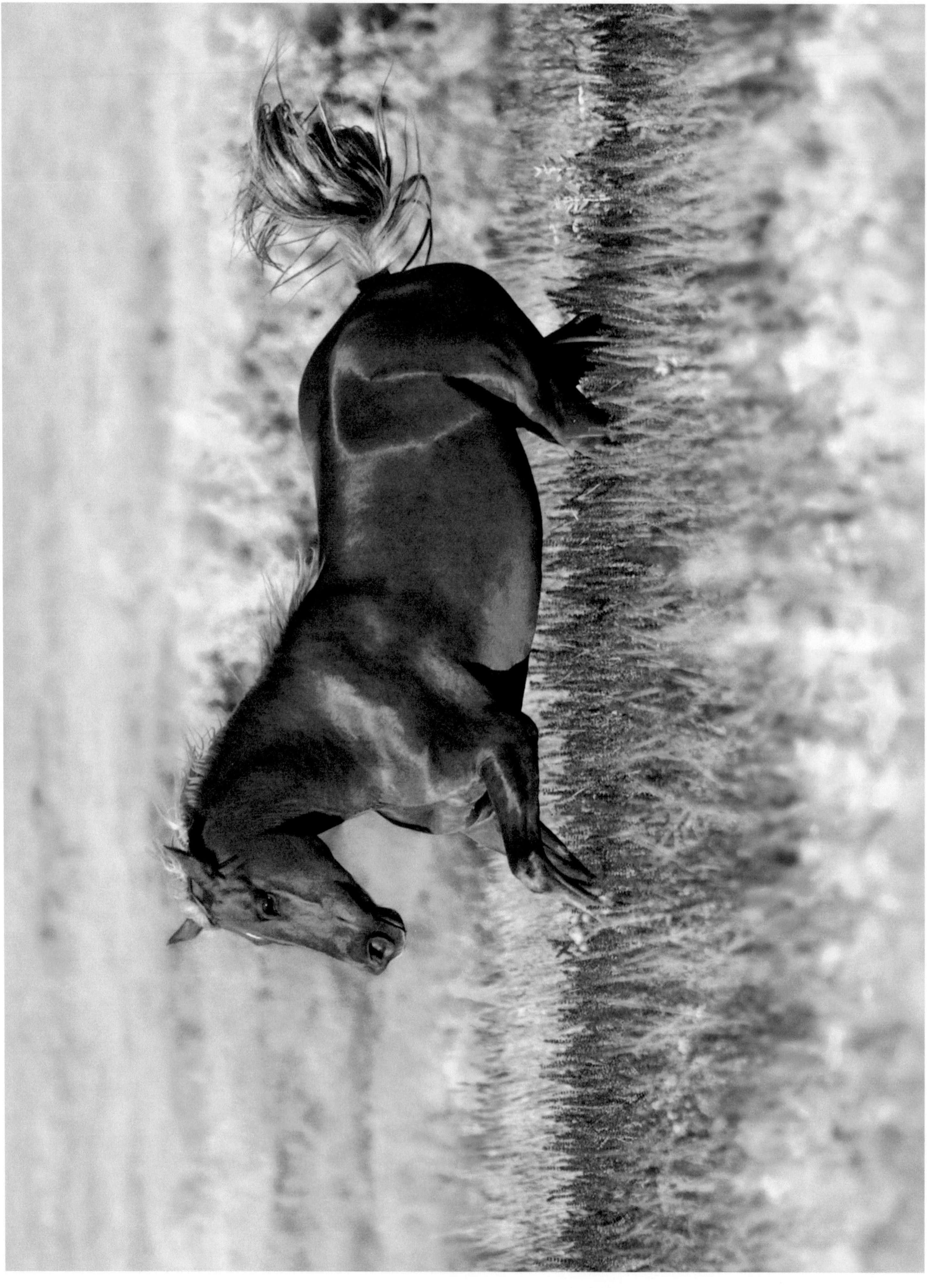

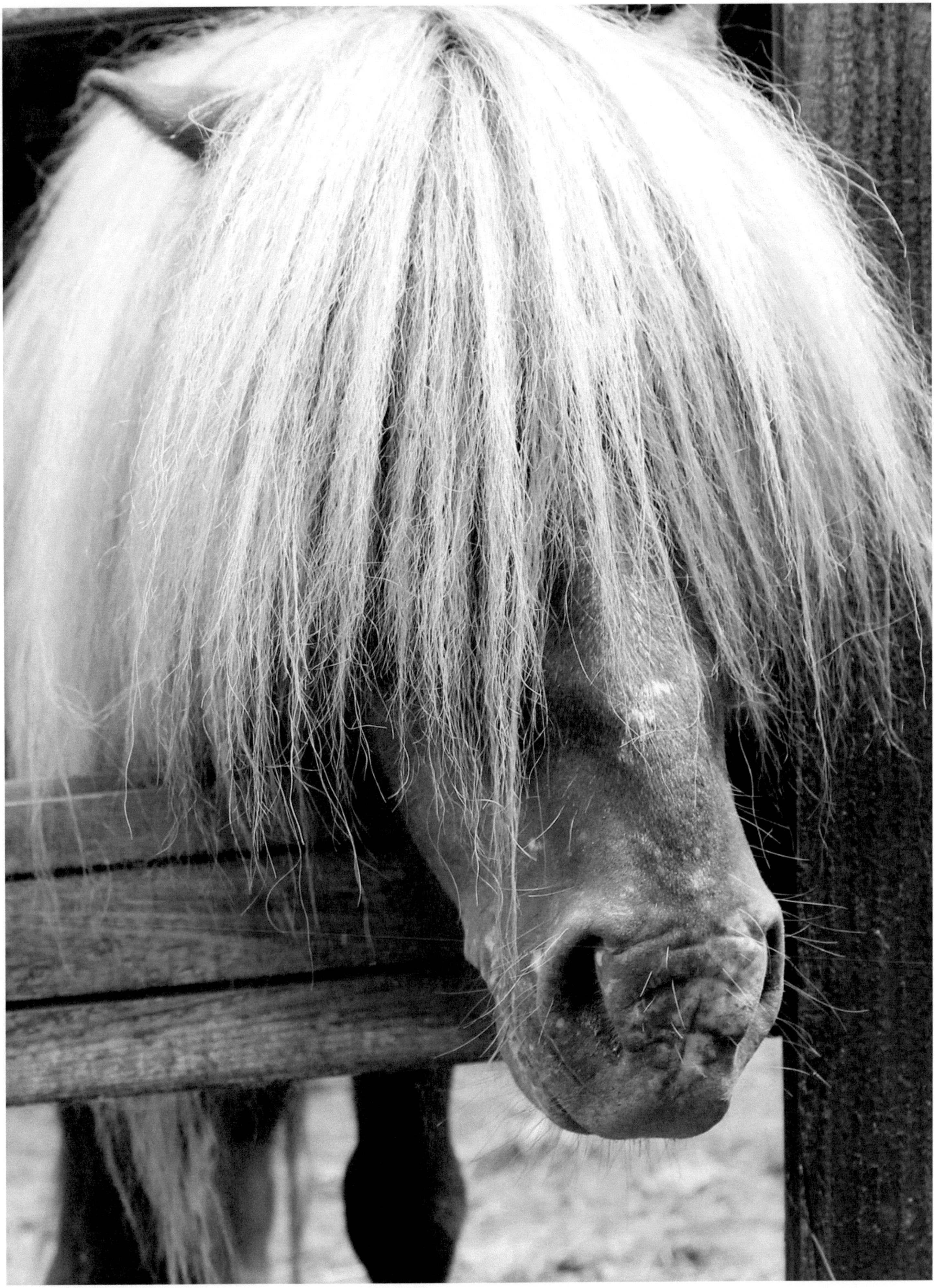

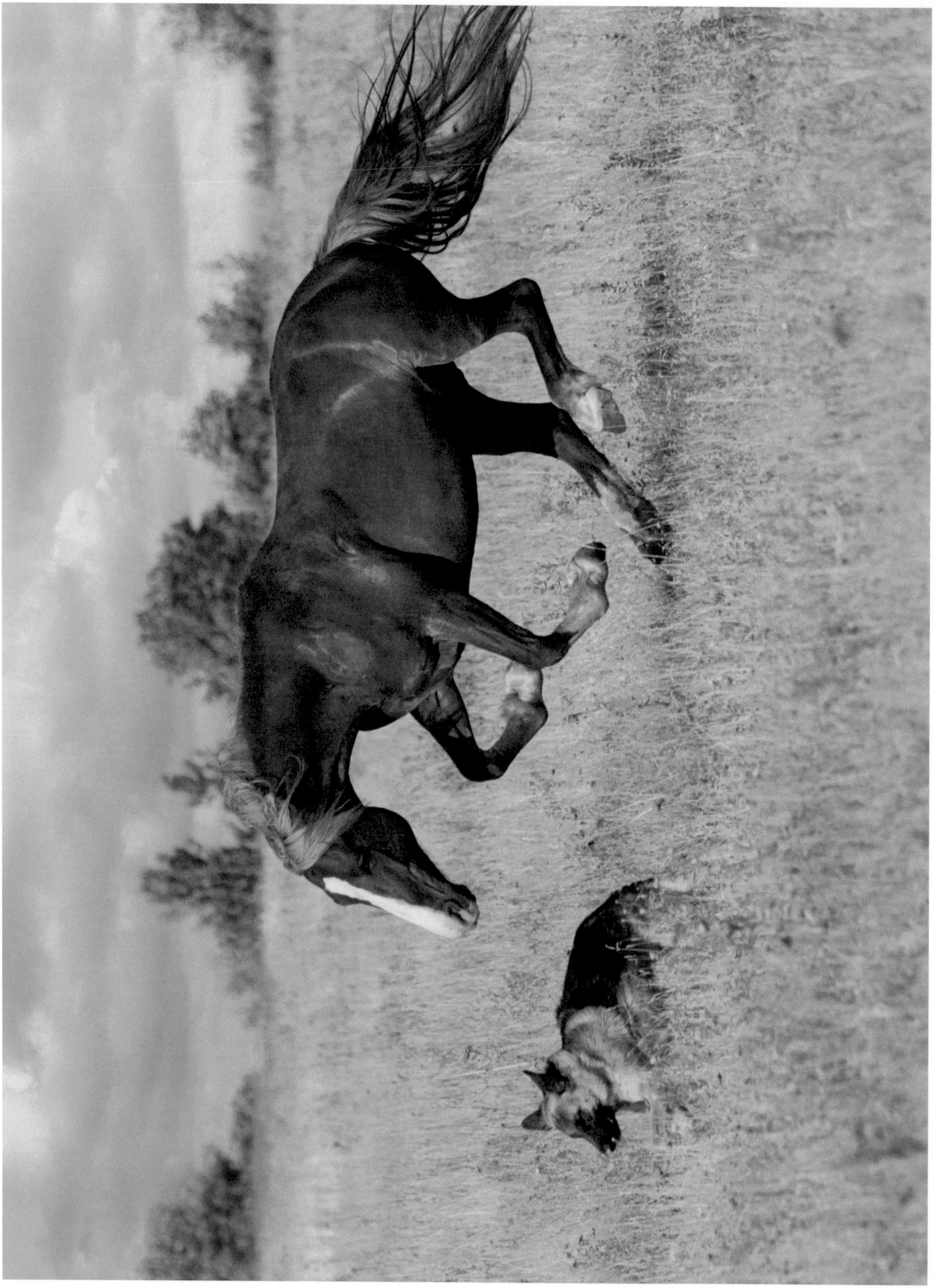

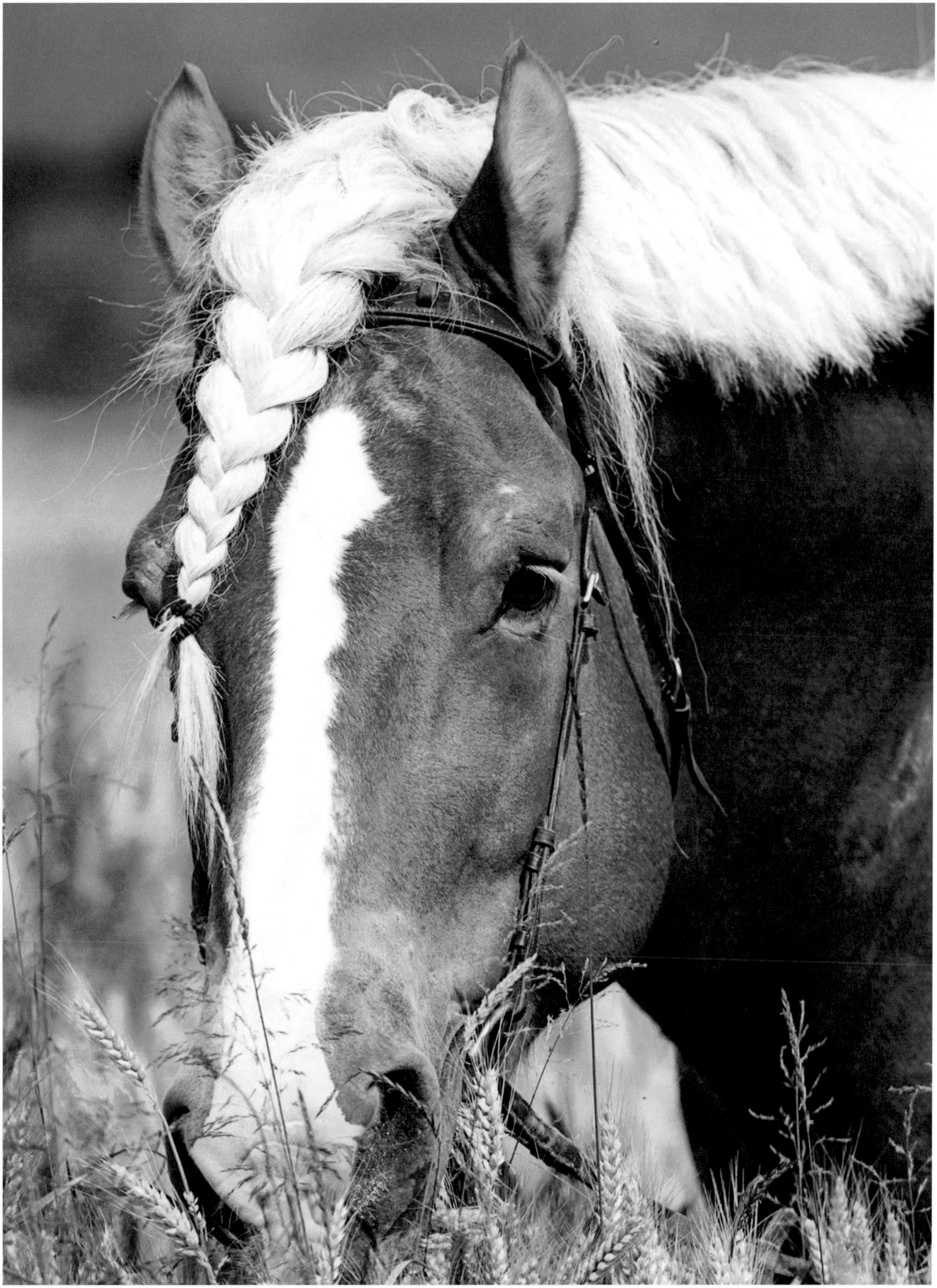

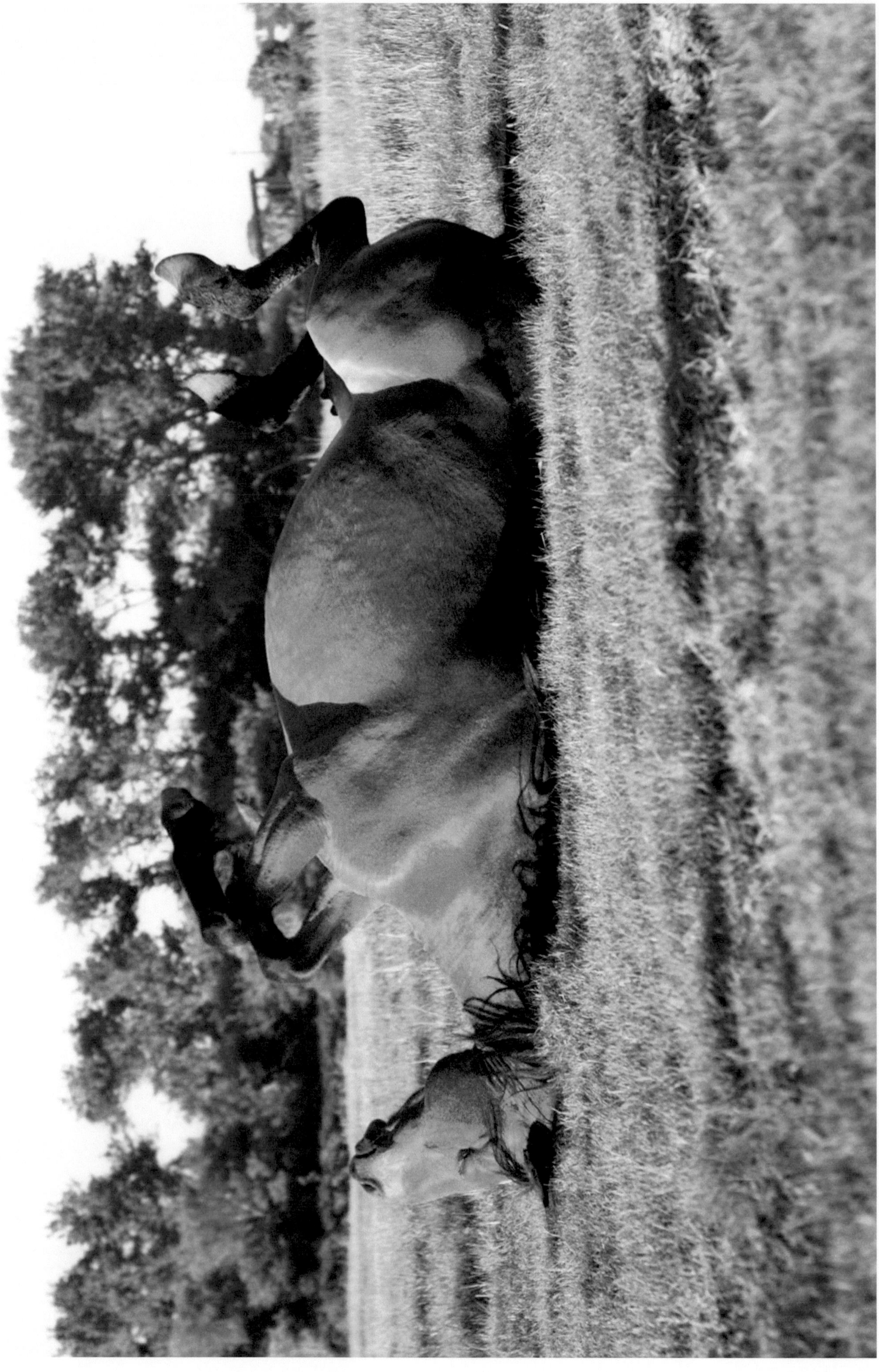

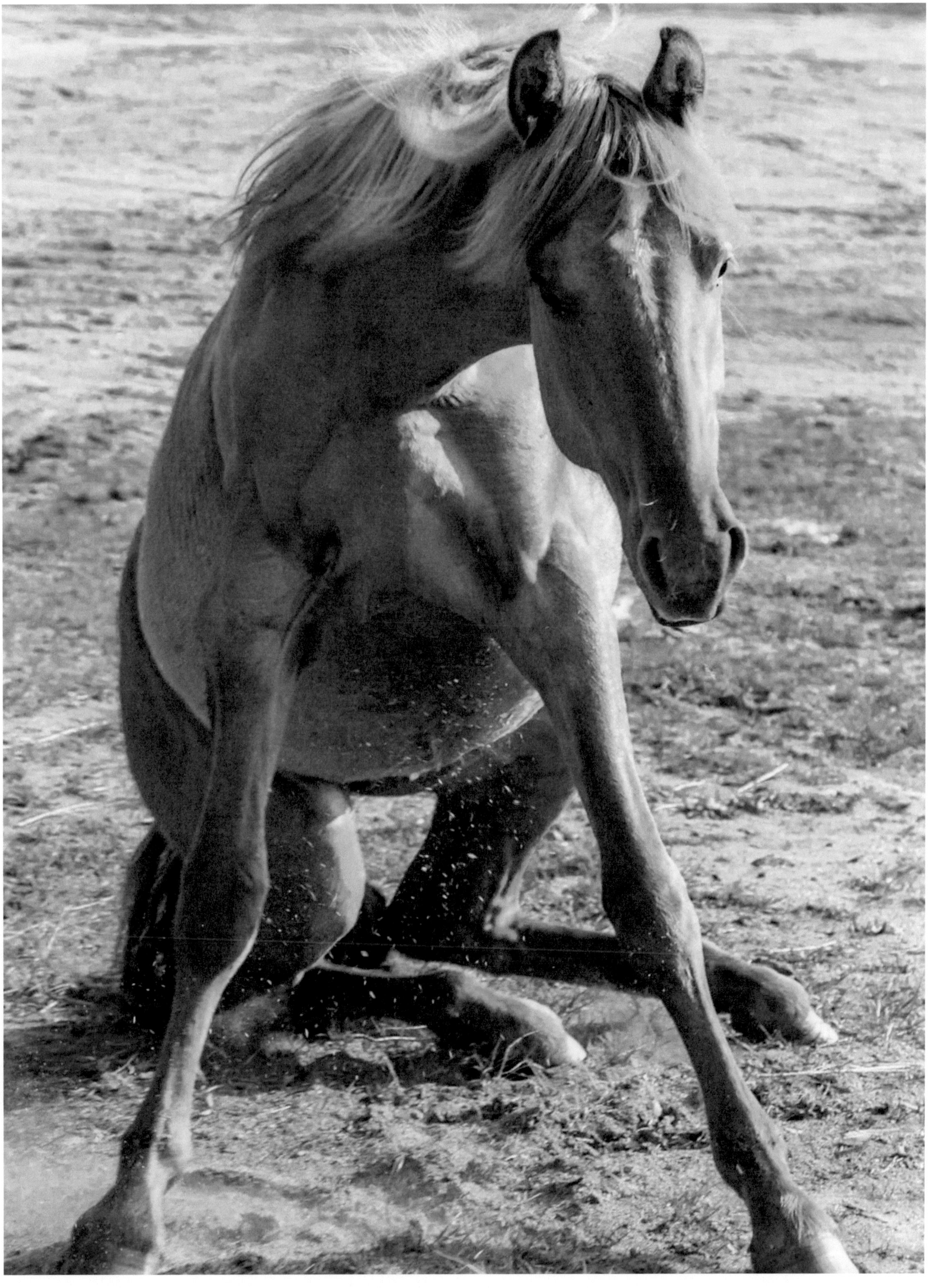

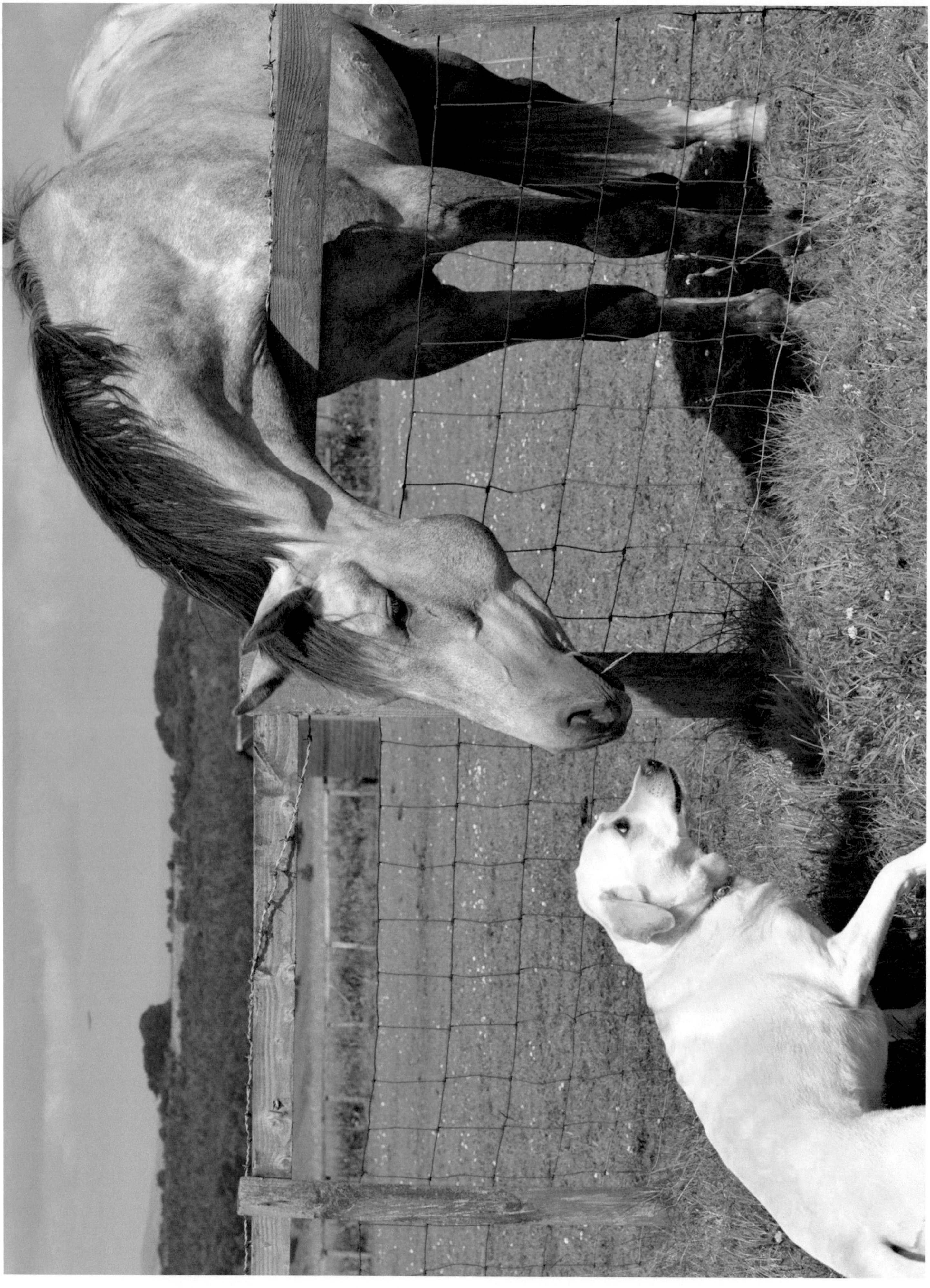

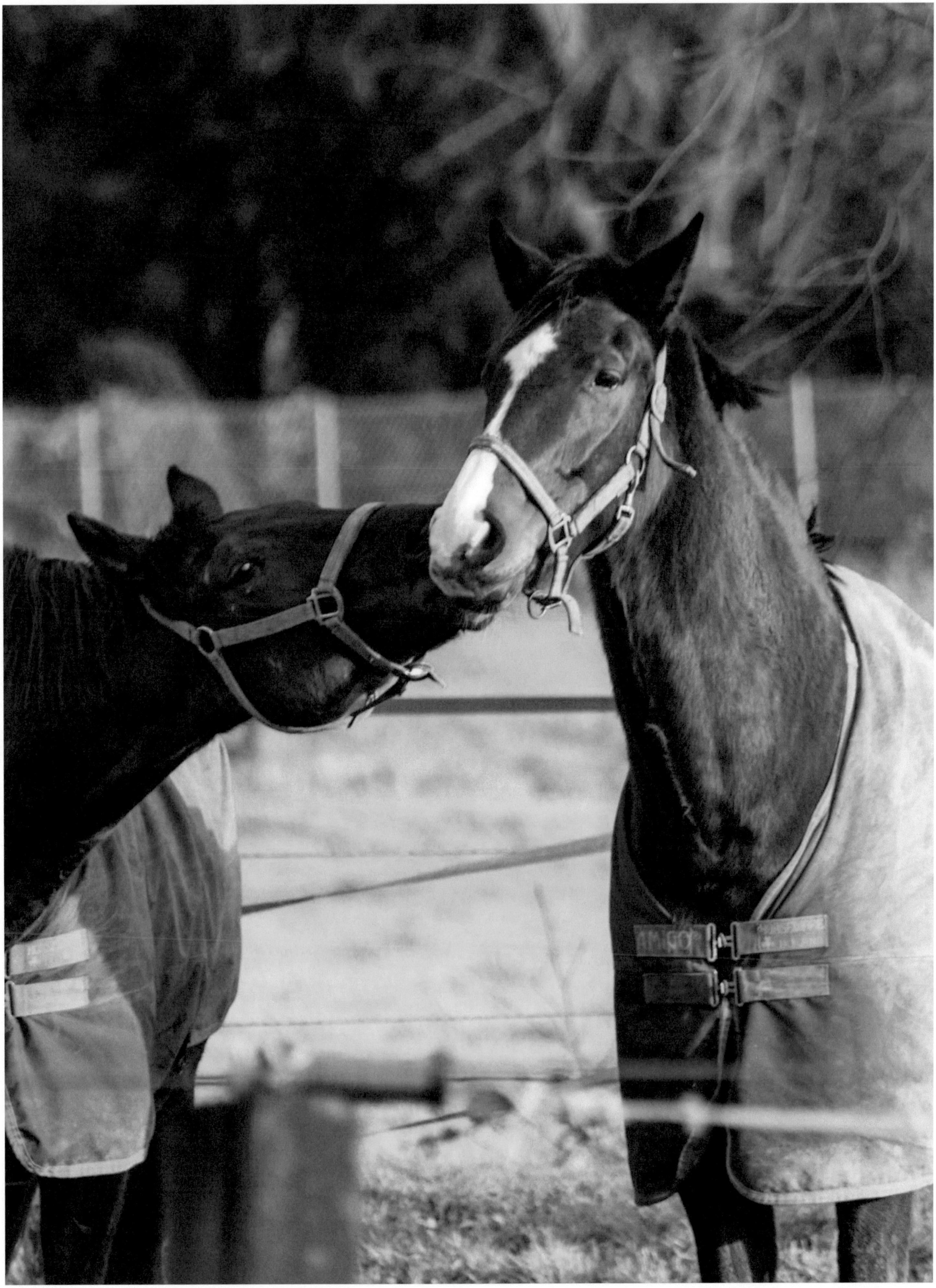

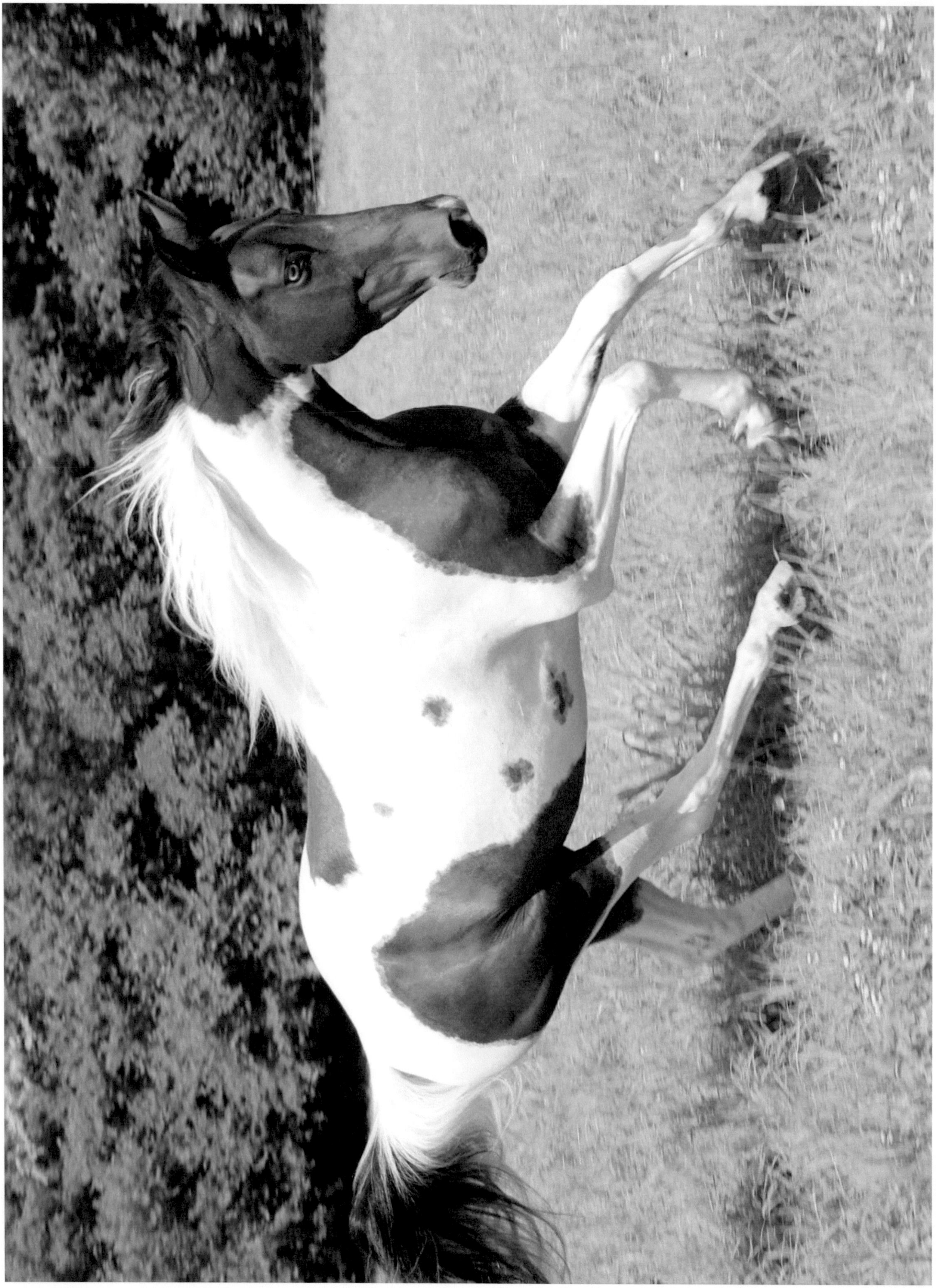

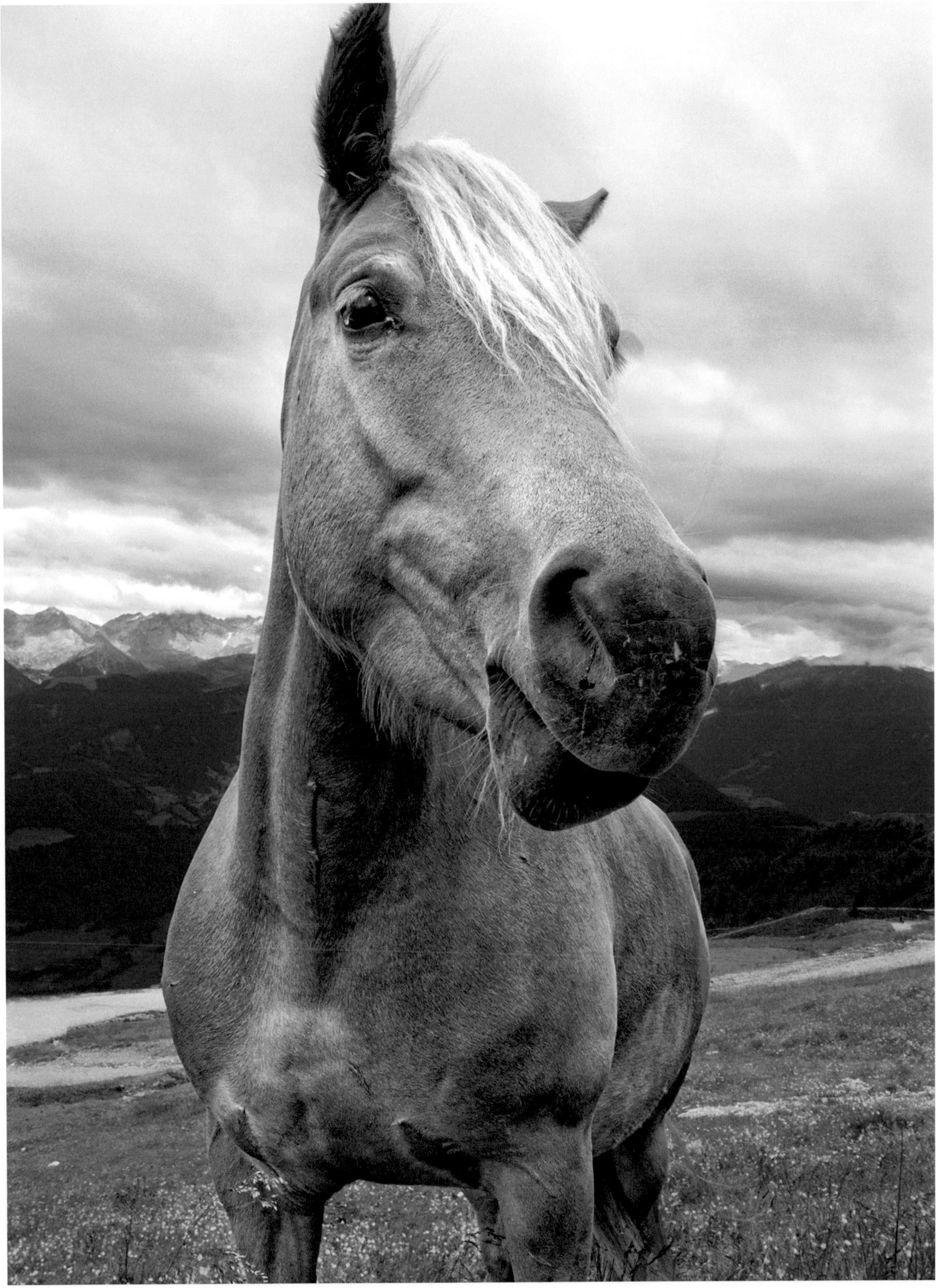

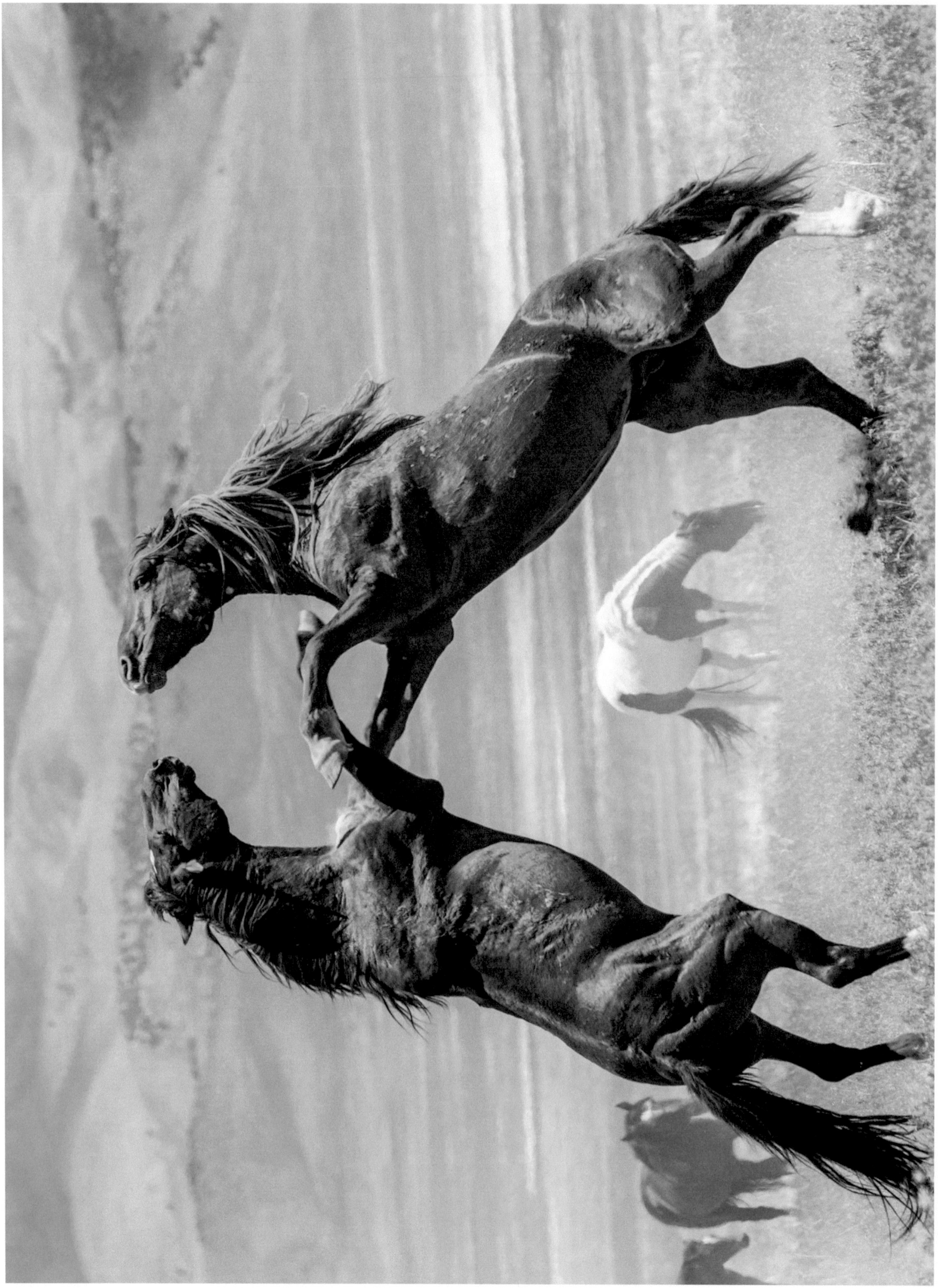

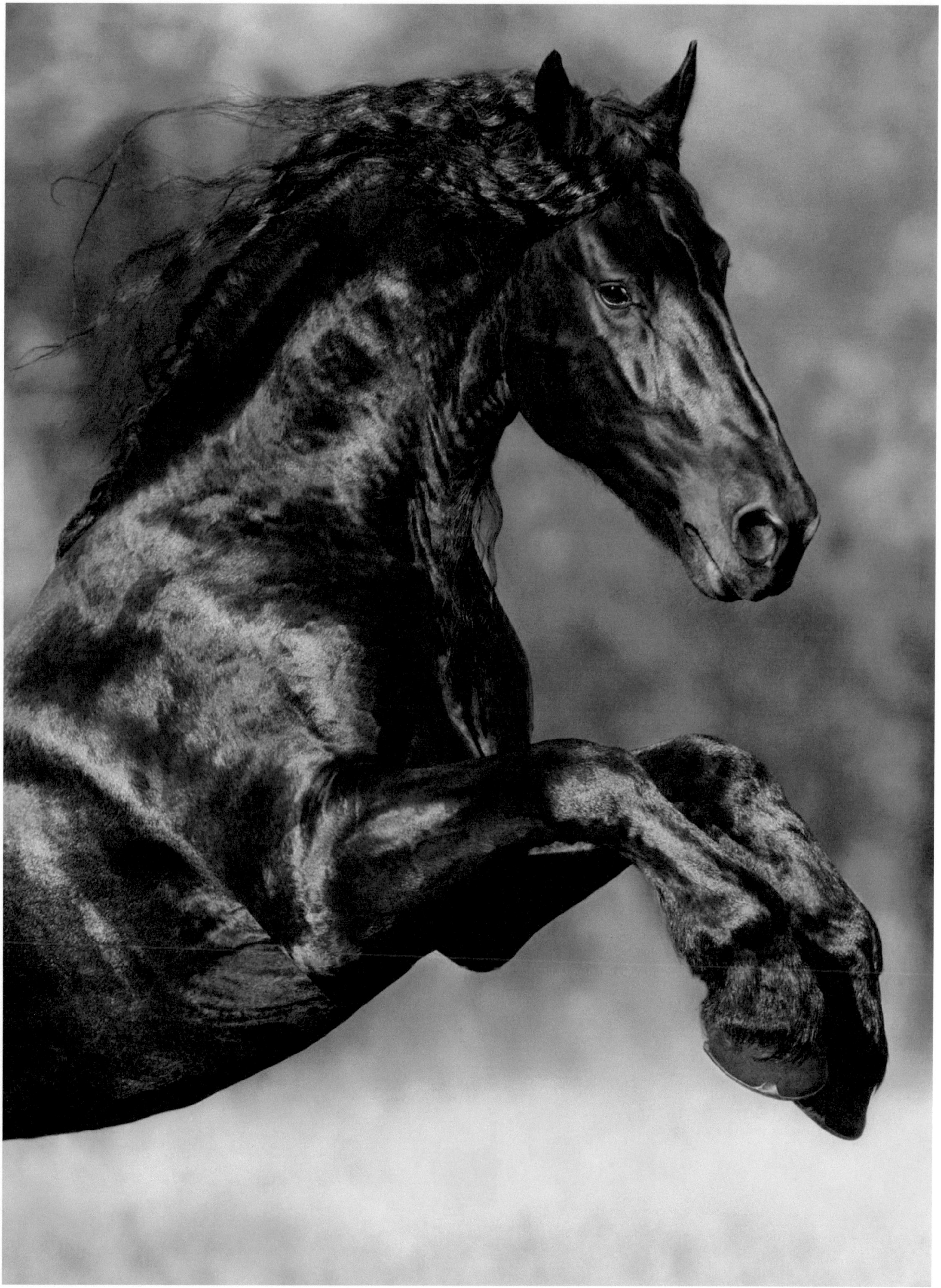

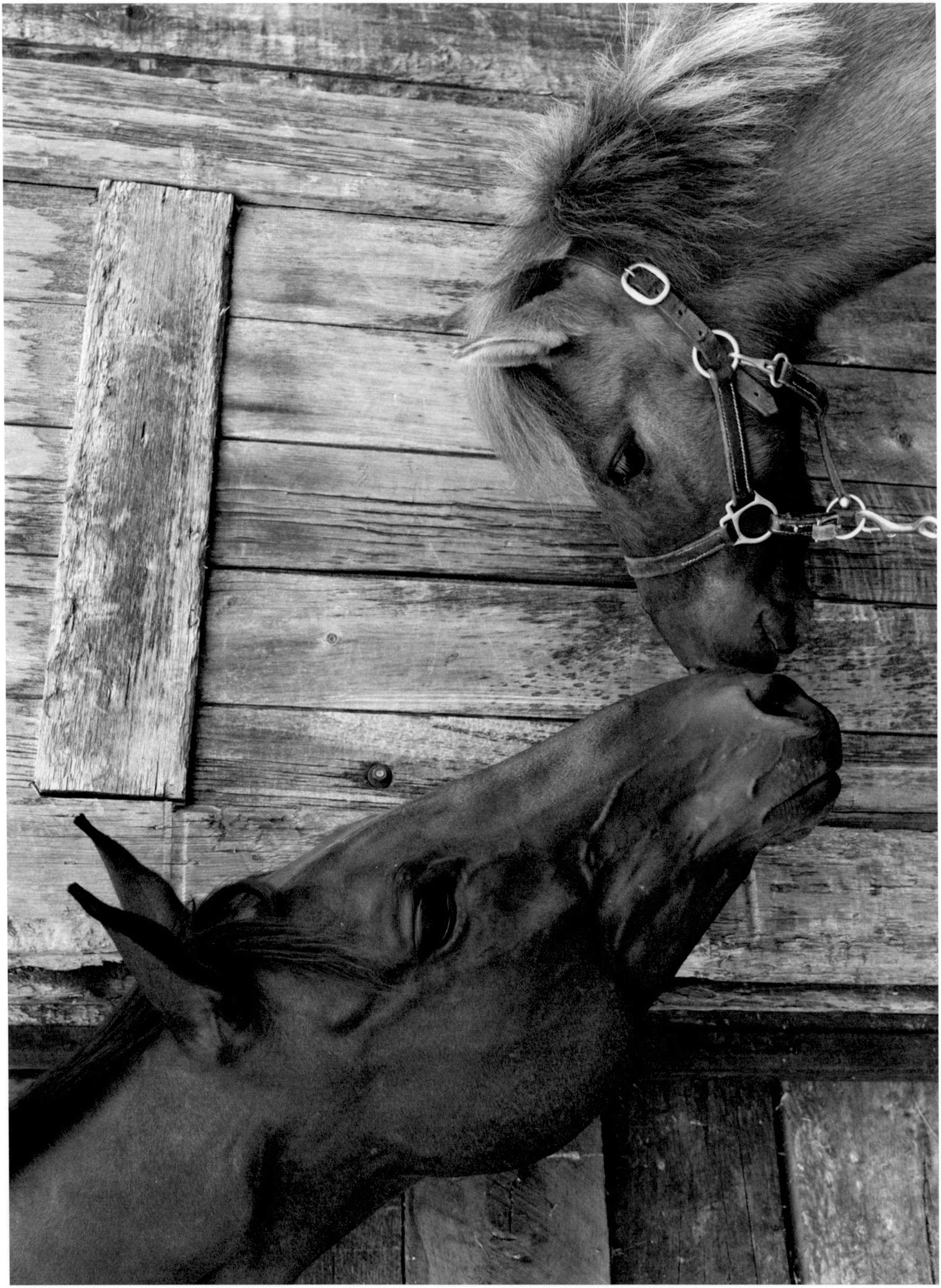

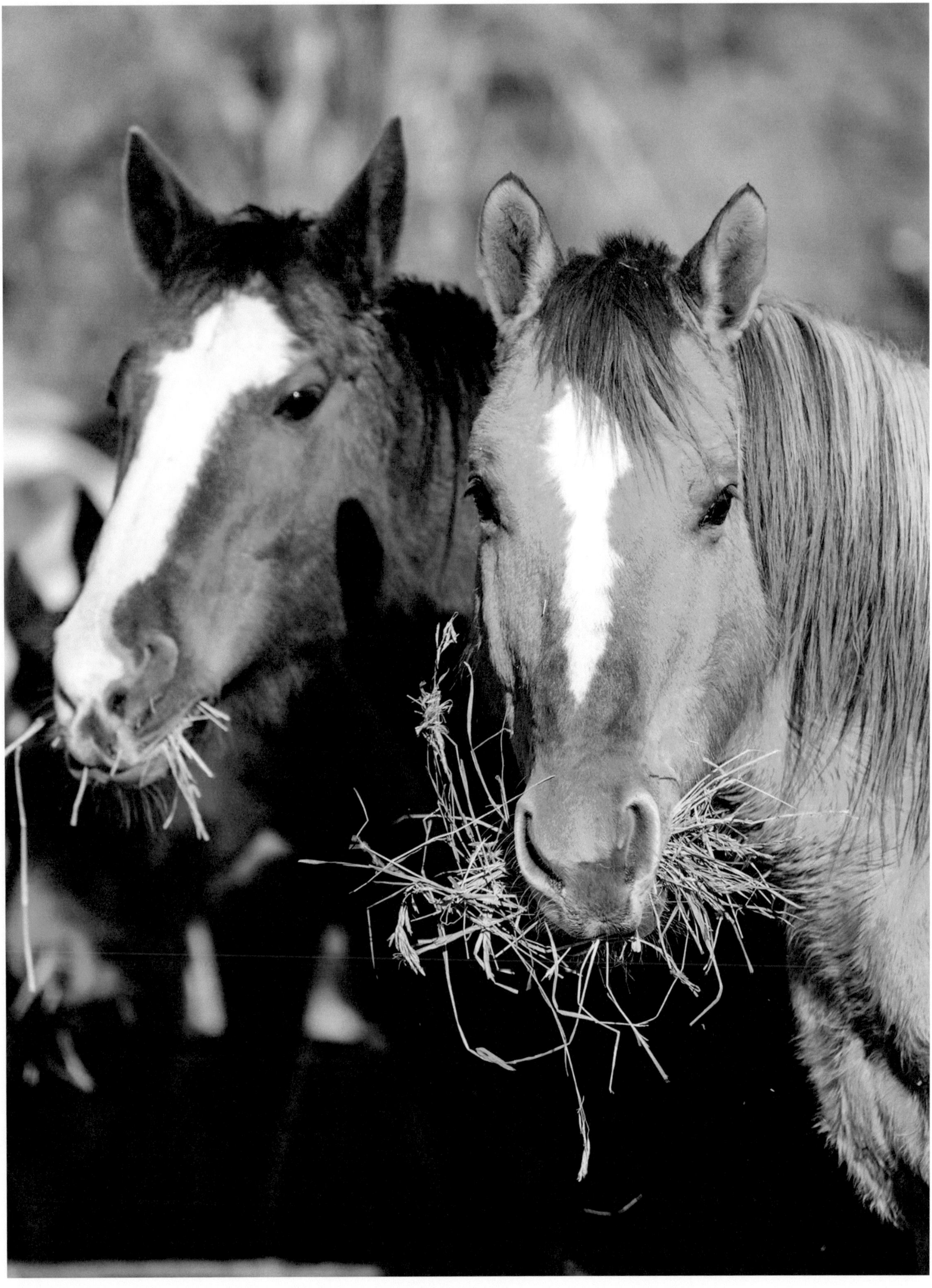

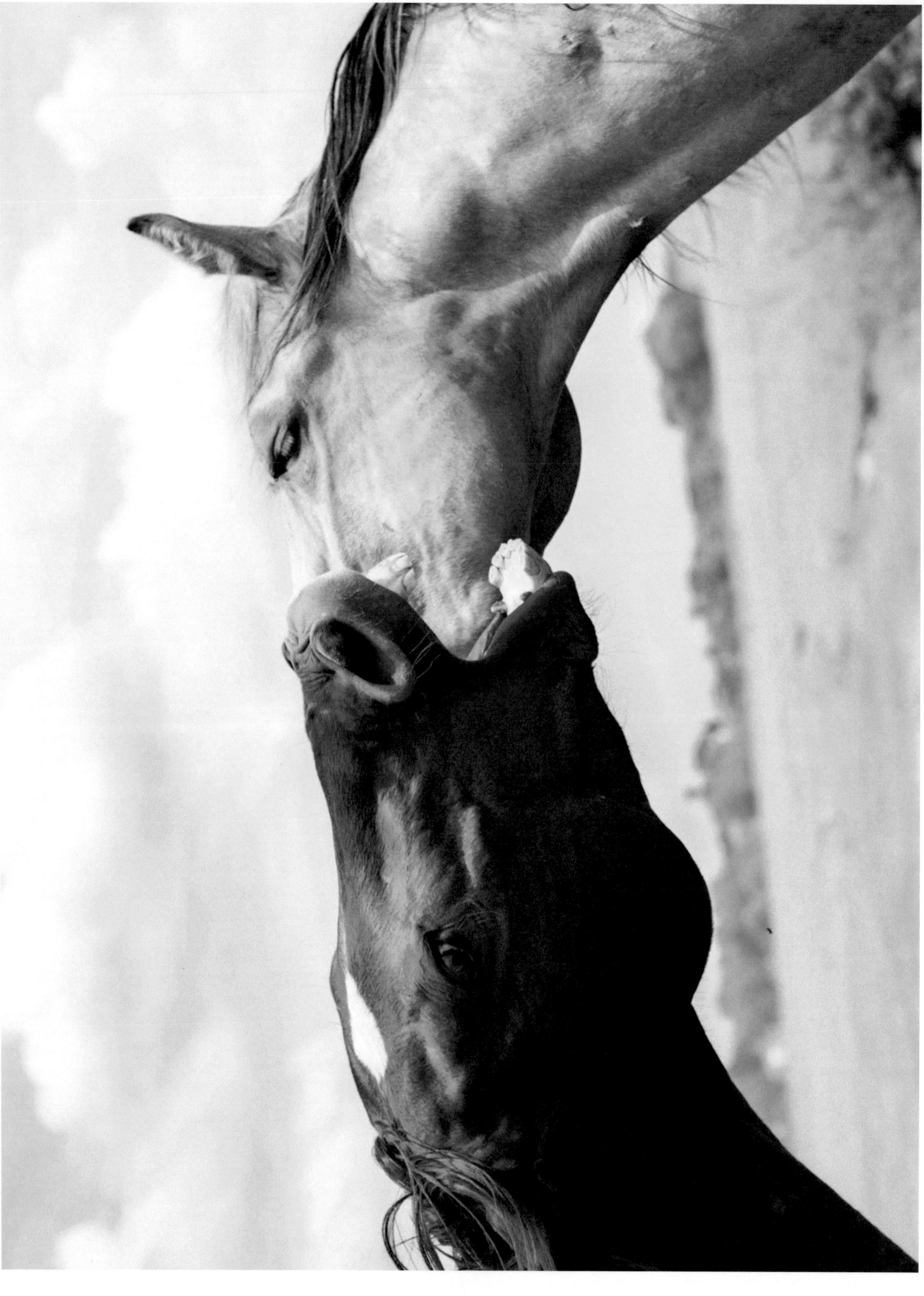

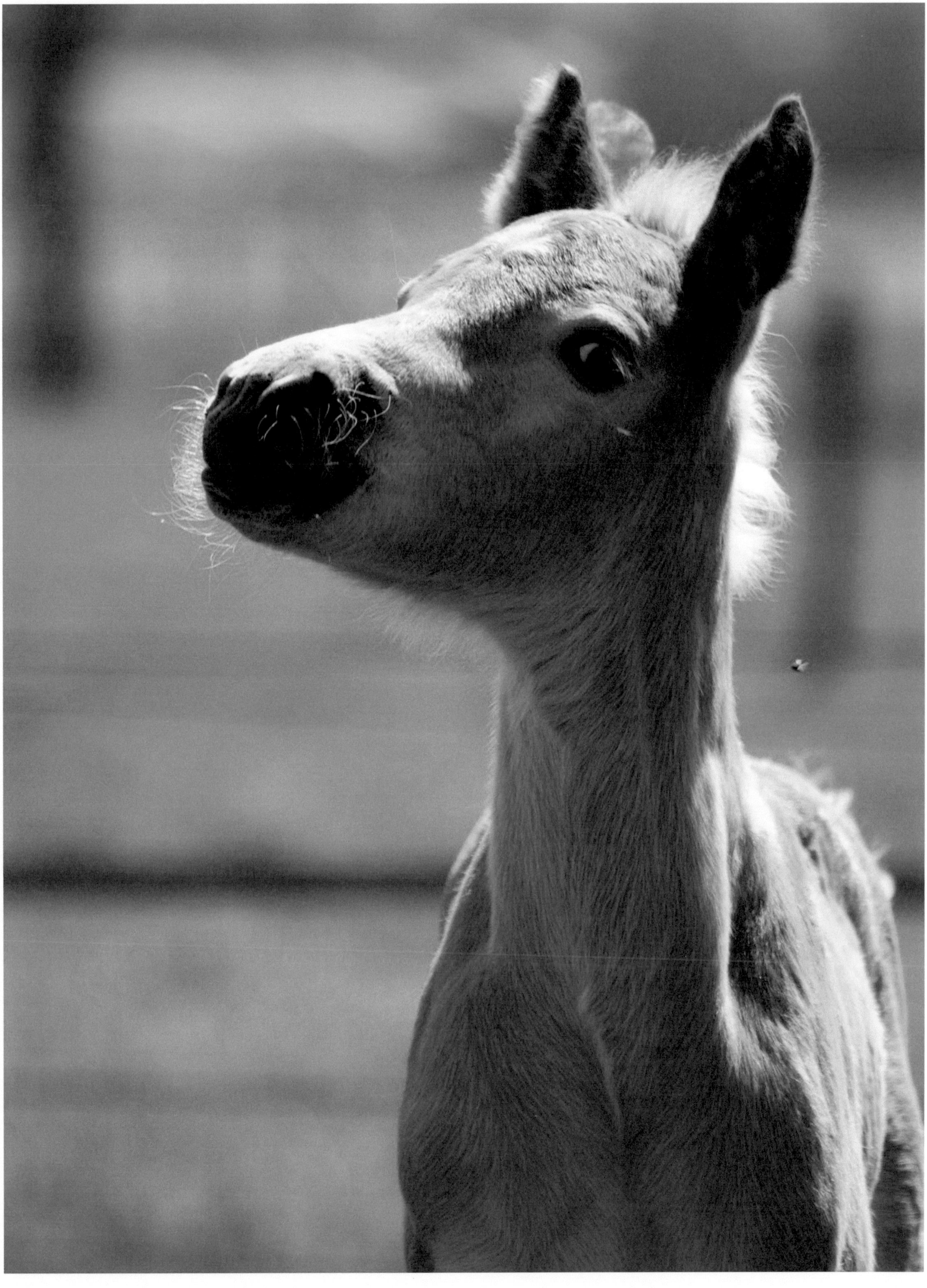

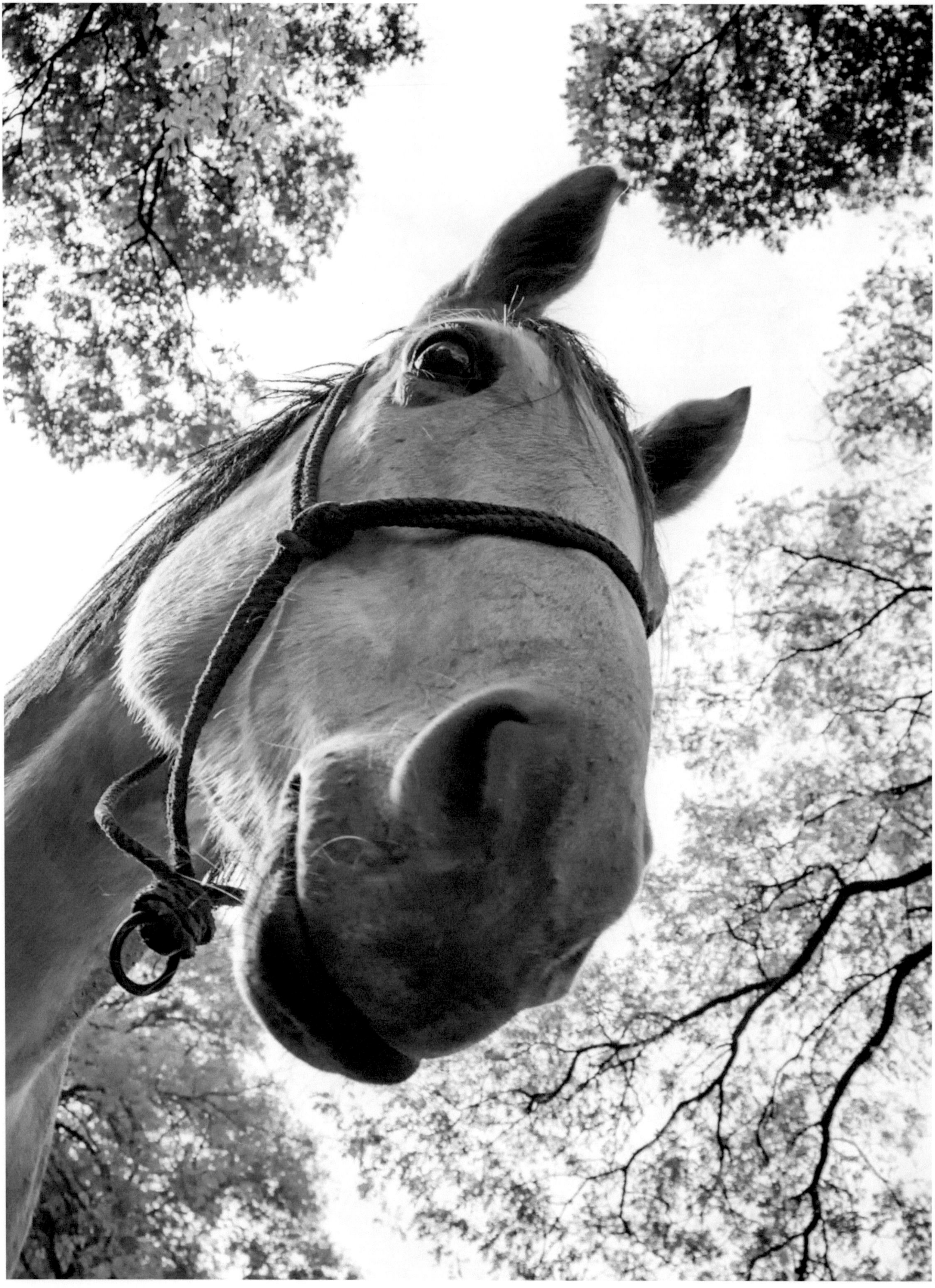

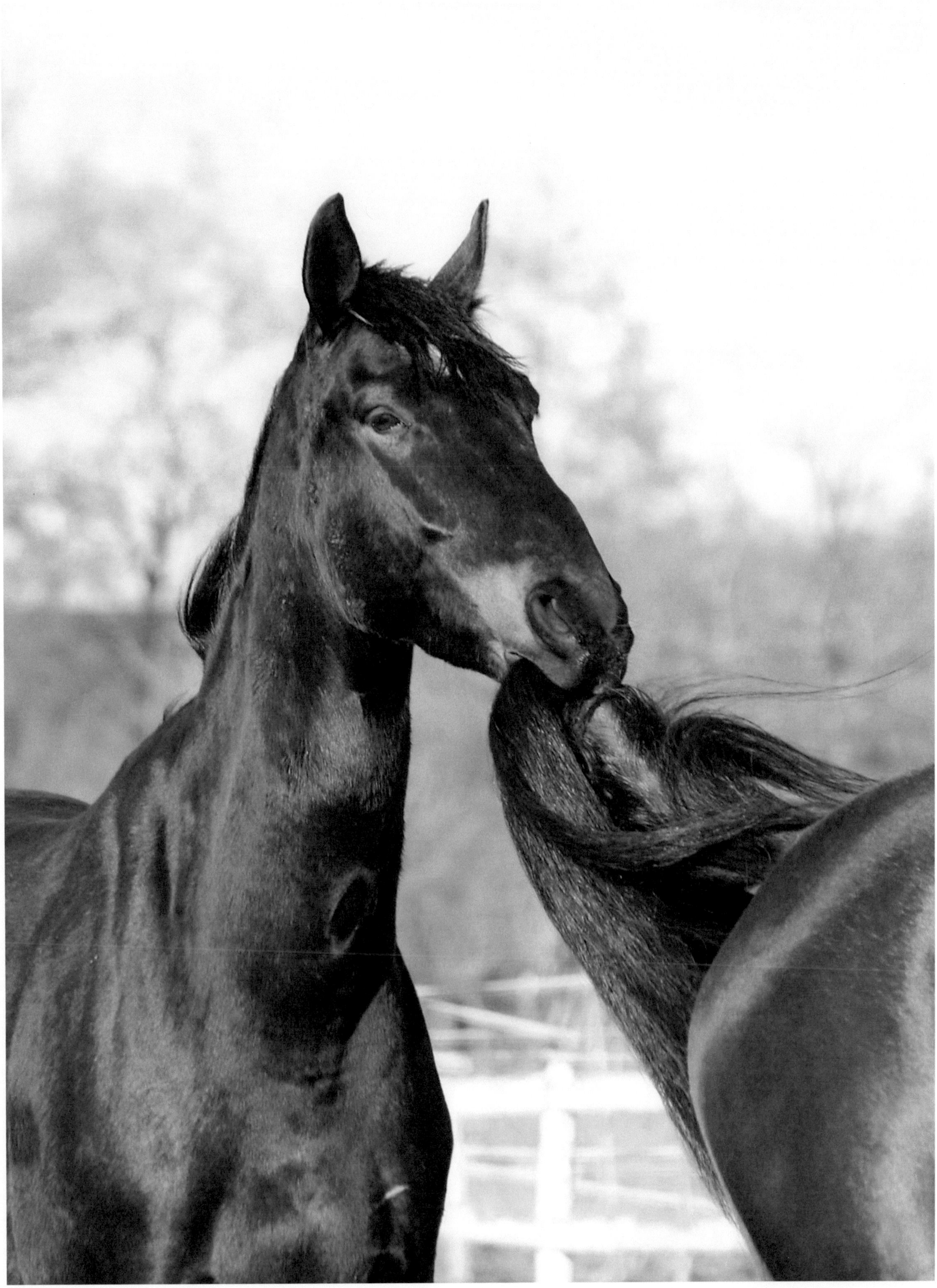

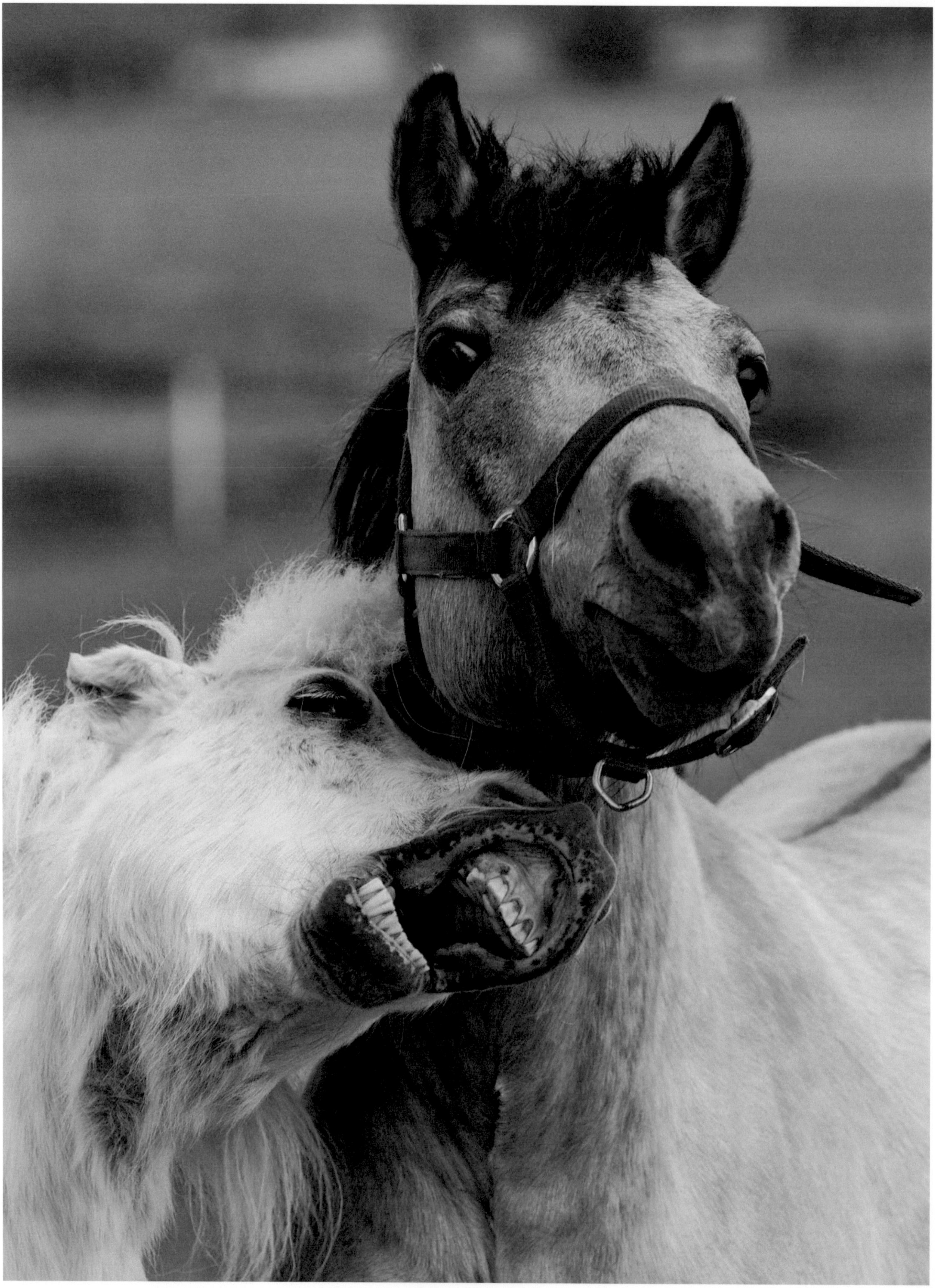

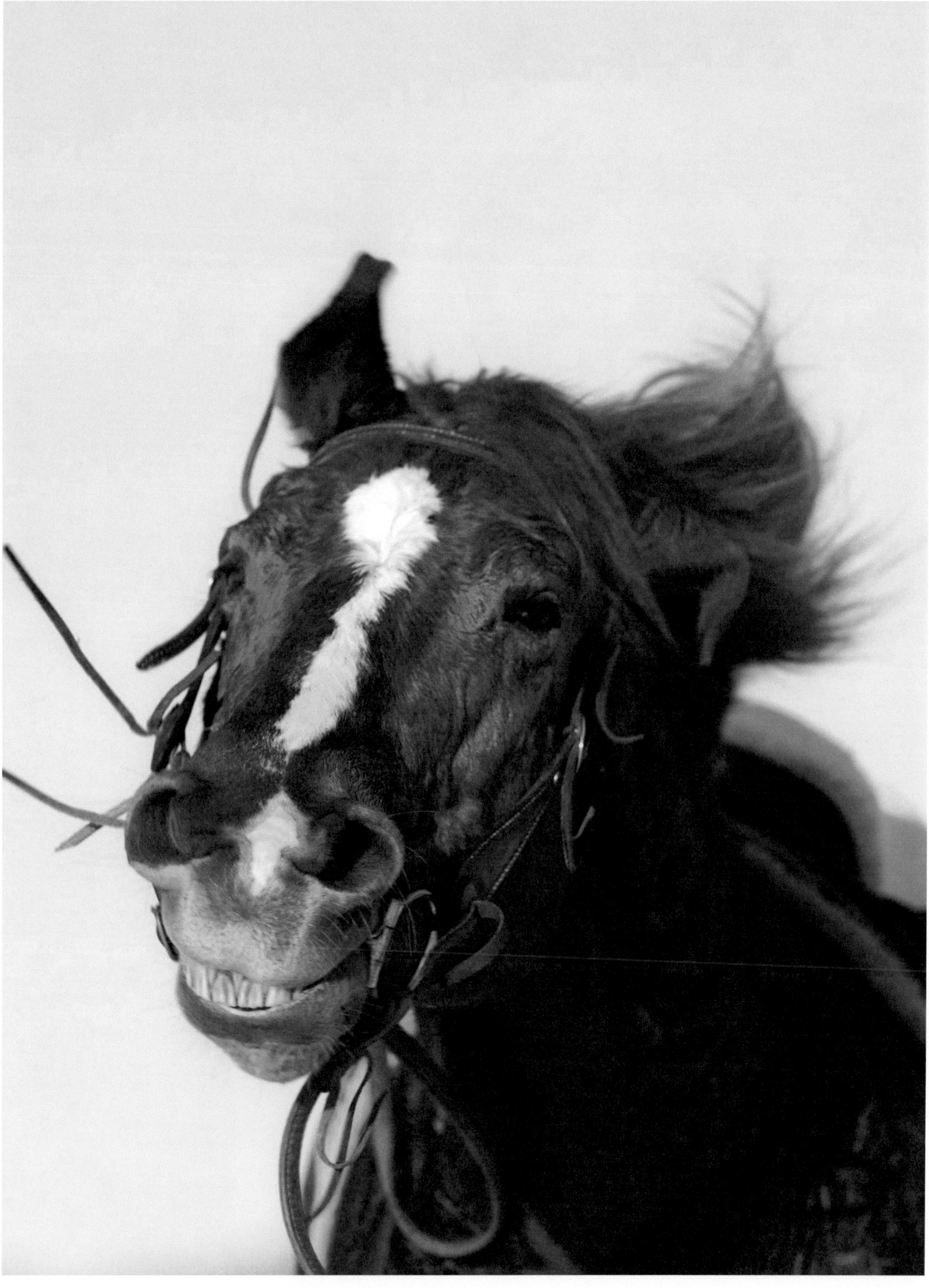

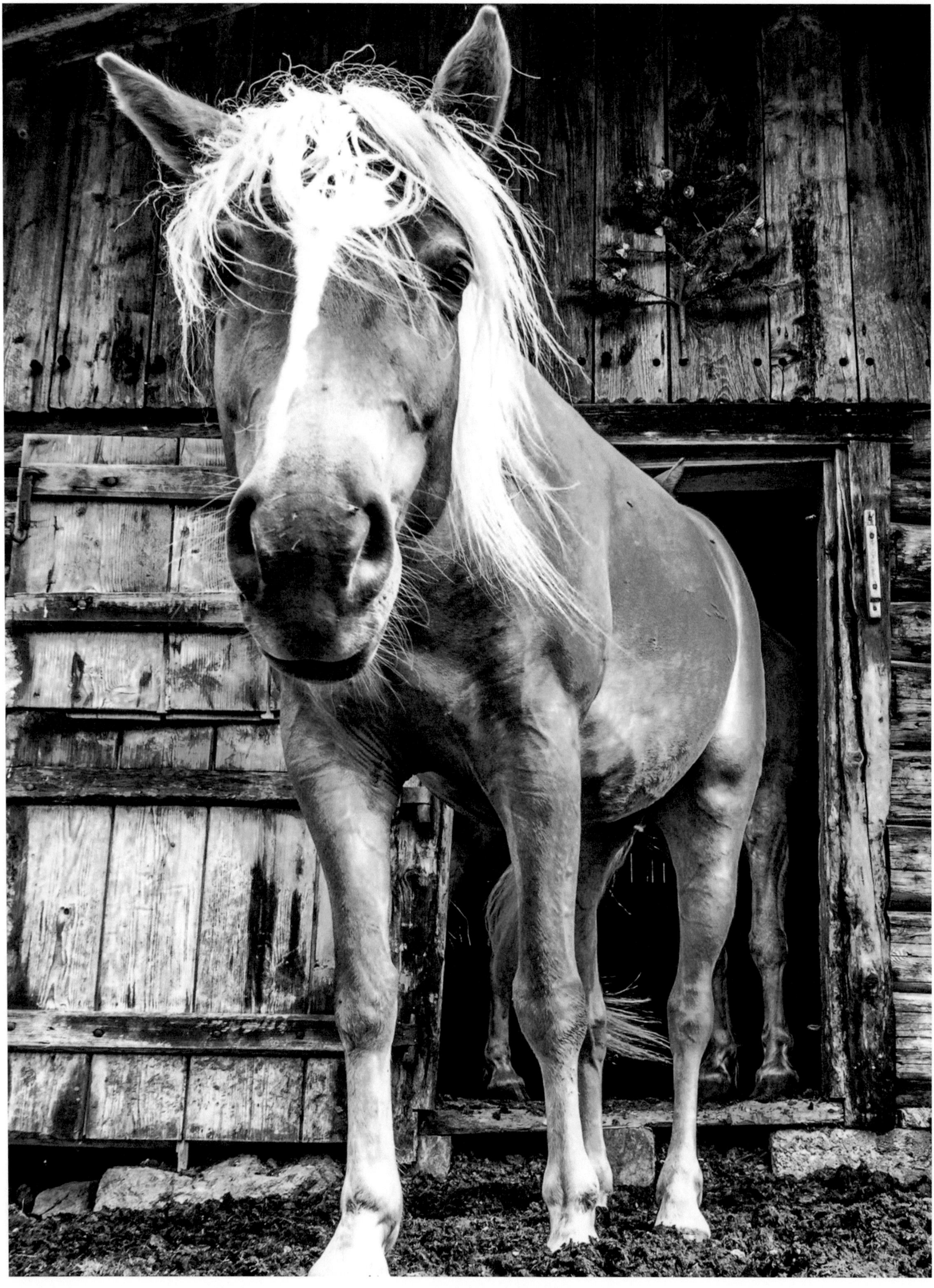

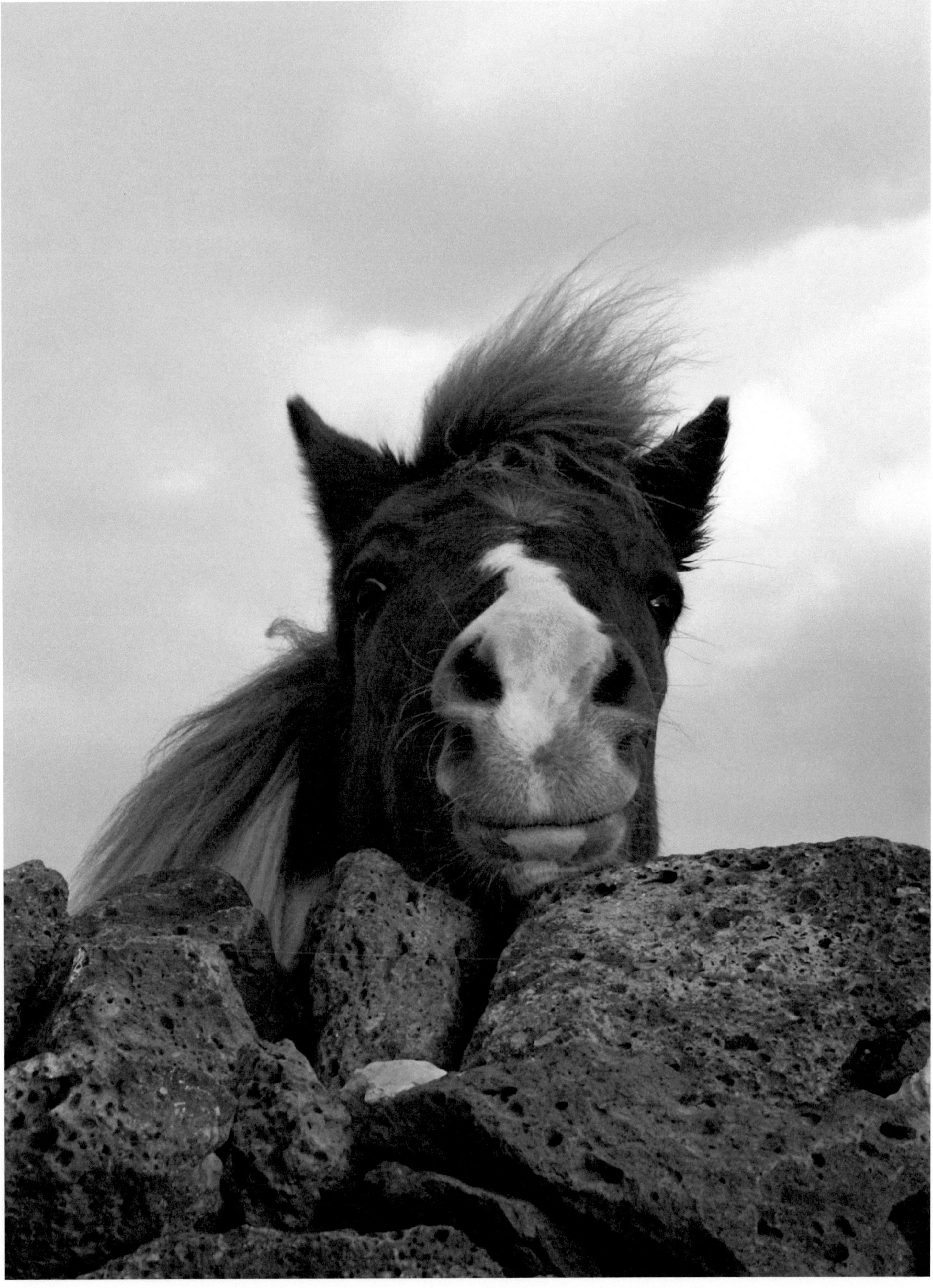

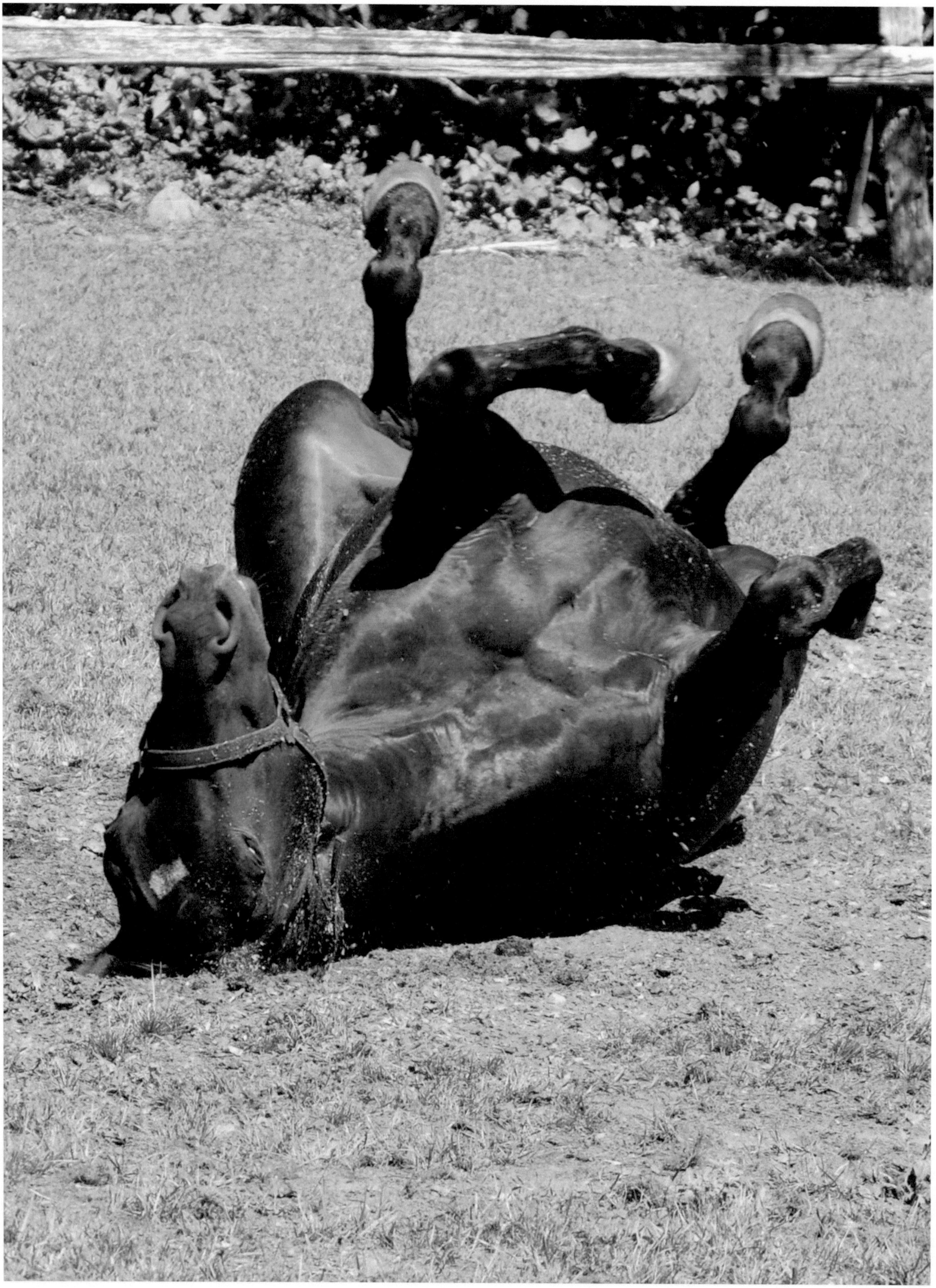

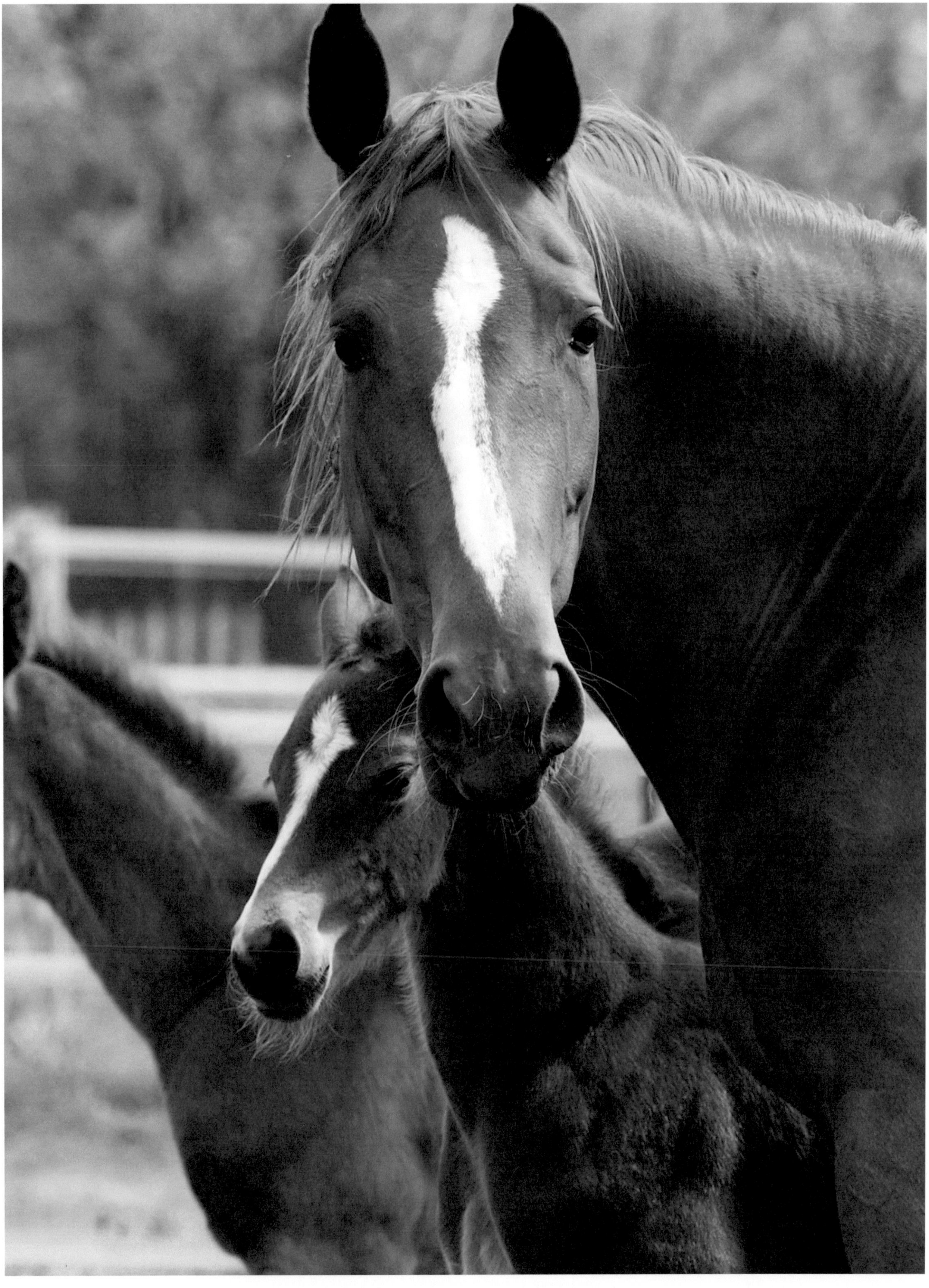

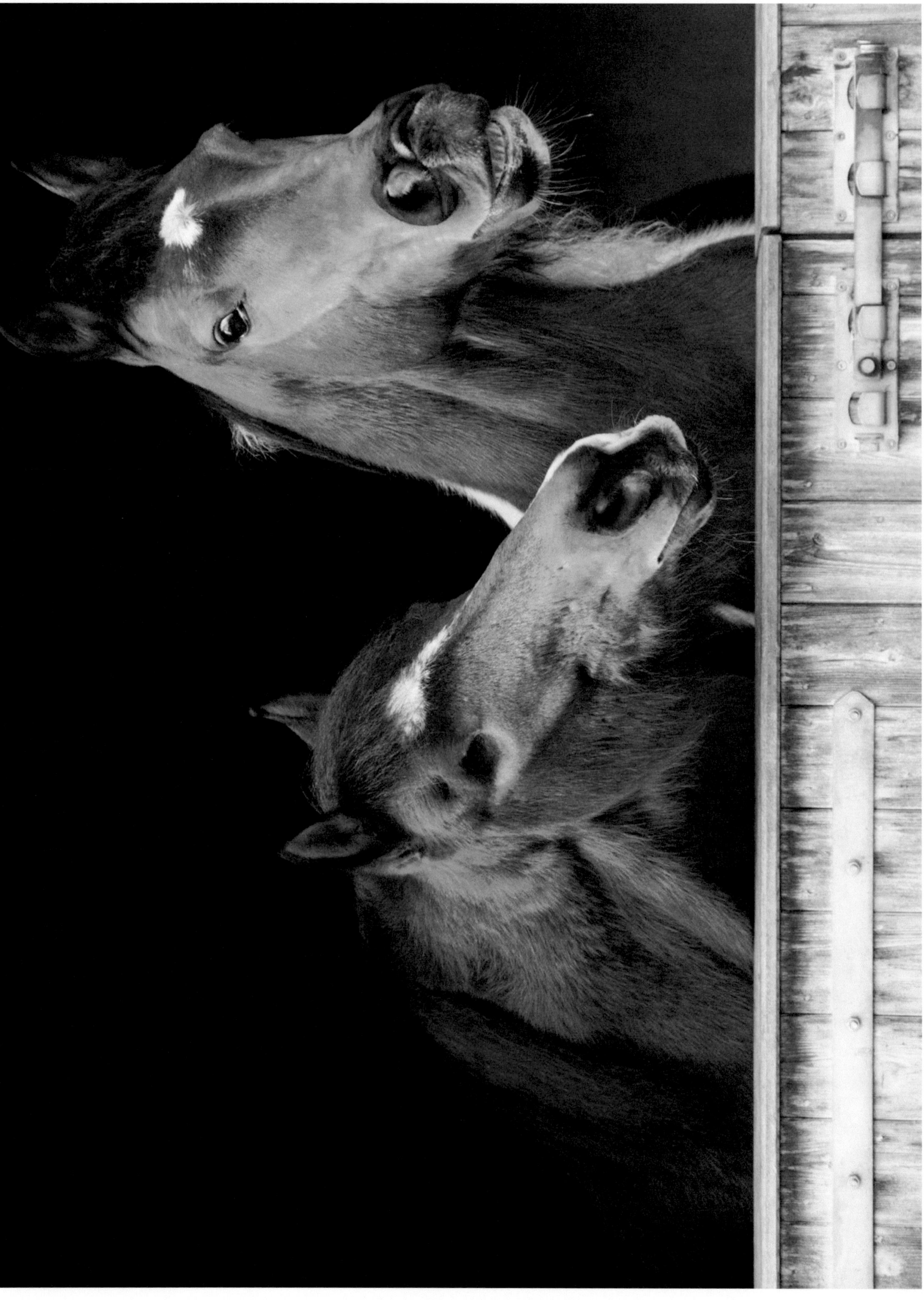

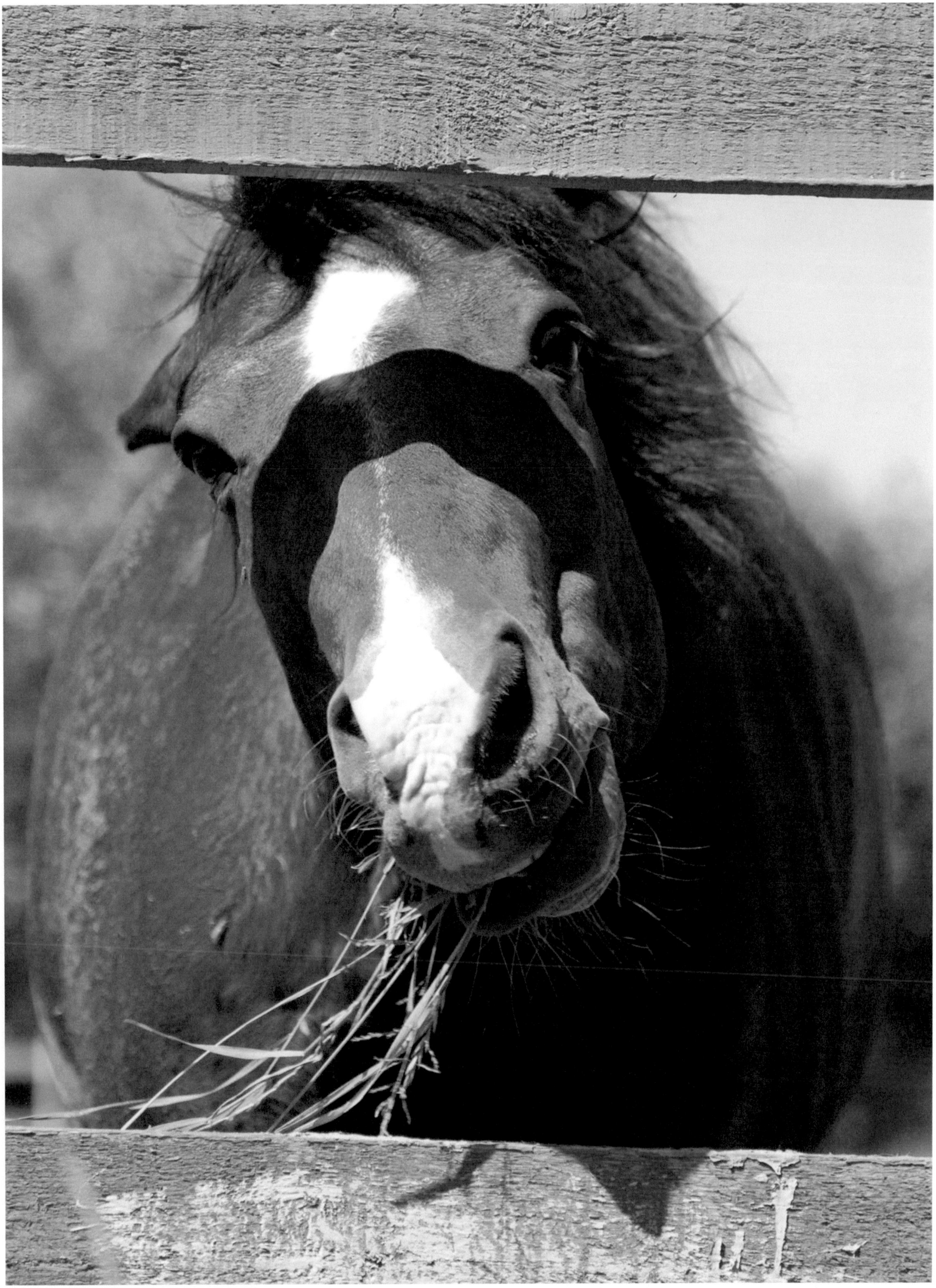

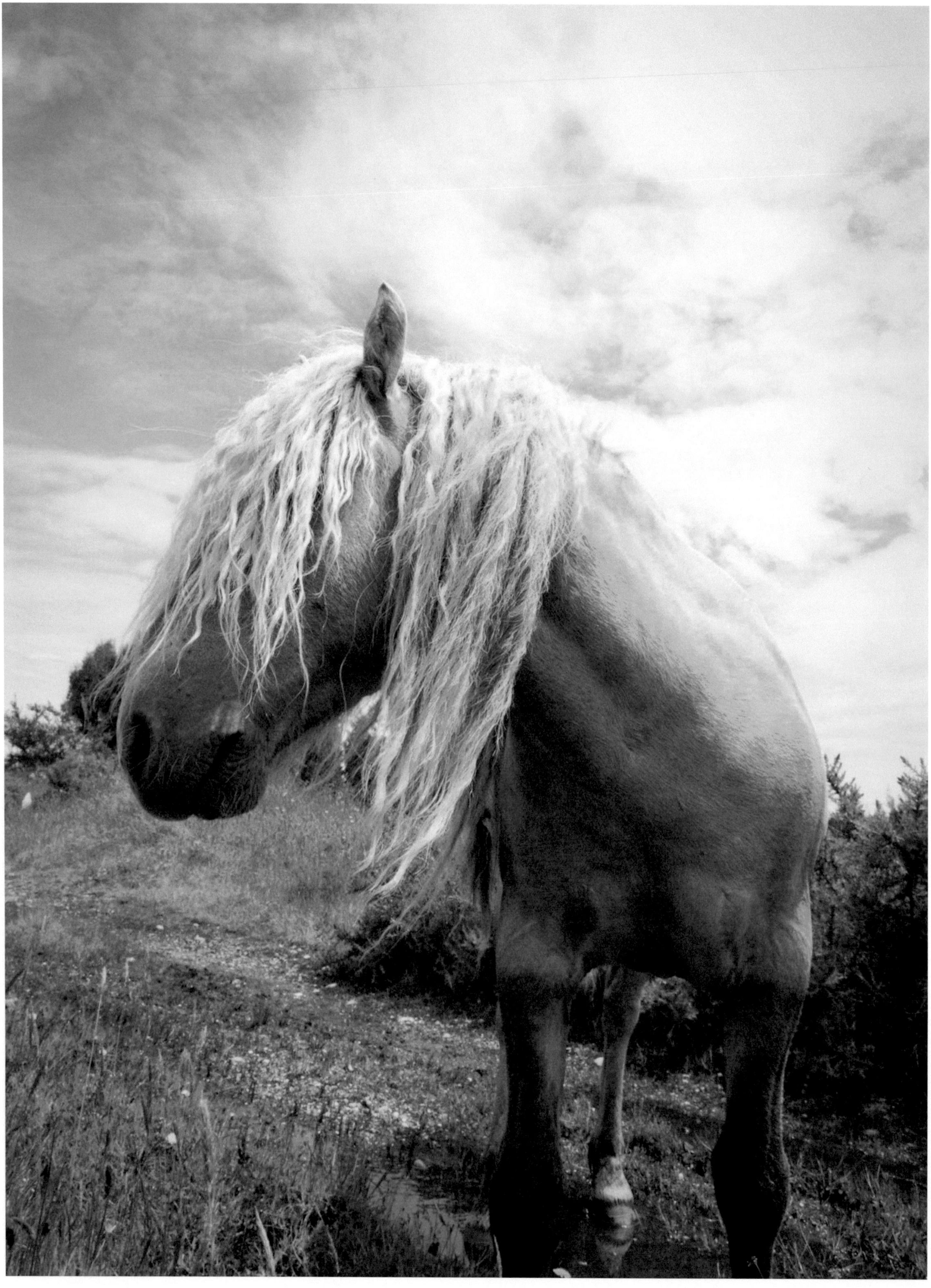

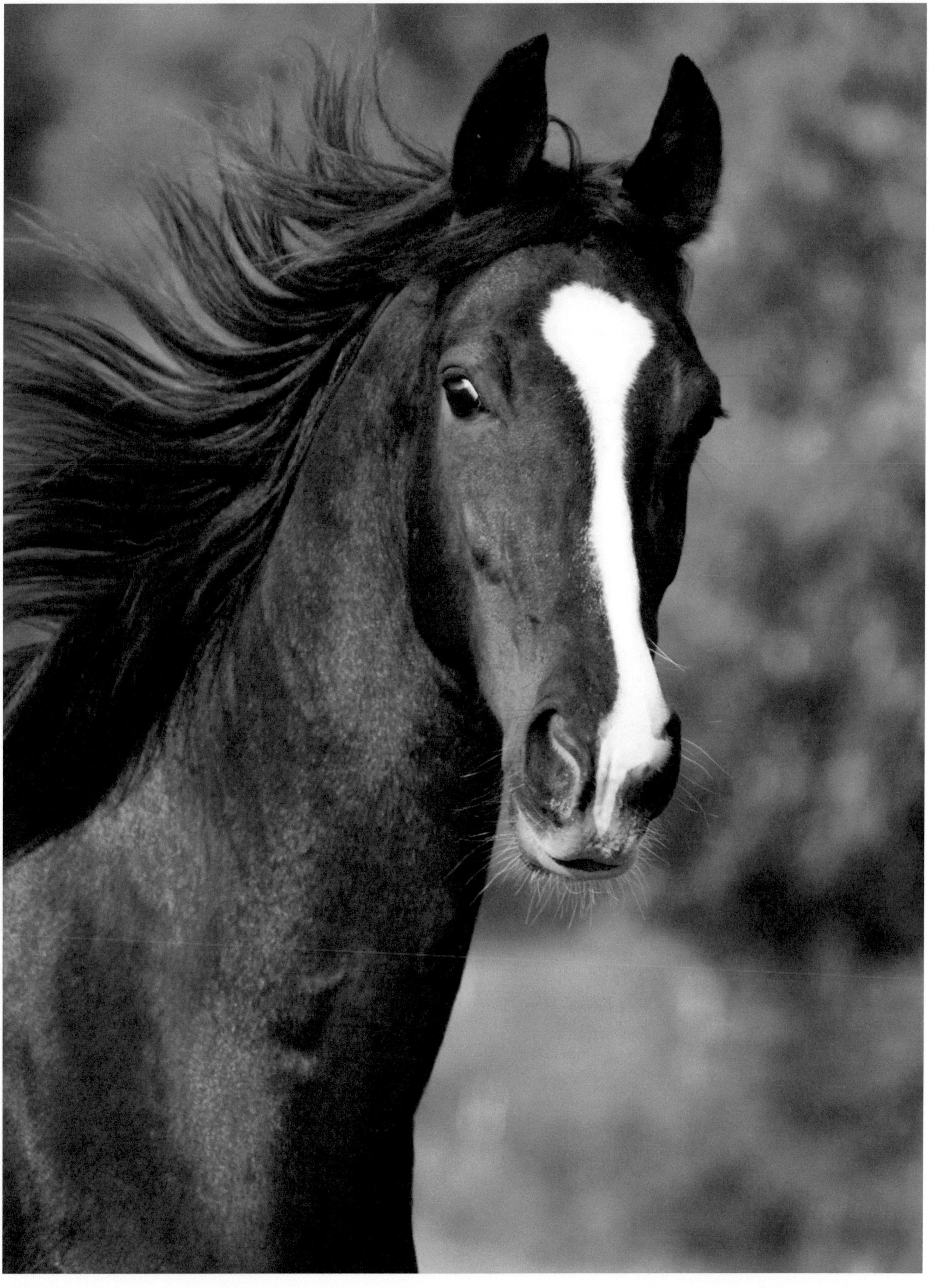